Ideas in Progress
Marxism and Radical Social Thought

Ideas in Progress

Bernard Ransom

Connolly's Marxism

First published 1980 by Pluto Press Limited,
Unit 10 Spencer Court, 7 Chalcot Road, London NW1 8LH

ISBN 0 86104 308 1
Cover designed by Richard Hollis GrR
Photoset by Photobooks (Bristol) Limited,
28 Midland Road, St Philips, Bristol

Printed in Great Britain by
The Camelot Press Limited, Southampton

Contents

Preface

This study does not presume to be a definitive analysis of James Connolly's standpoint as a marxist thinker and activist. It is rather offered as an interpretation of Connolly, an argument based upon my own research and upon the work of other scholars. My general indebtedness to the work of others is indicated in the chapter references, but I would like to record at the outset a special recognition of the pioneering contributions made to Connolly scholarship by Desmond Greaves, Owen Dudley Edwards and Manus O'Riordan. None of them would agree wholly with the interpretation offered here, but their works are vital sources for all who would seek a serious understanding of Connolly.

A special word of thanks is due to Mike Milotte and Bob Purdie for their helpful comments on earlier drafts and to Richard Kuper of Pluto Press, for his patient encouragement during the prolonged writing process. (Needless to say none of them is in any way responsible for my conclusions.) Finally, my supreme debt is to my wife, Toni, whose intellectual and moral support was vital to the entire enterprise.

Bernard Ransom
St John's
Newfoundland

December 1979

Abbreviations

BSP	British Socialist Party
CGT	Confederation Generale de Travail
ILP	Independent Labour Party
ILP(I)	Independent Labour Party of Ireland
IRB	Irish Republican Brotherhood
ISRP	Irish Socialist Republican Party
ITWU	Irish Transport Workers' Union
IWW	Industrial Workers of the World
OBU	'One Big Union'
SDF	Social Democratic Federation
SLP	Socialist Labor Party of America
SPA	Socialist Party of America
SPI	Socialist Party of Ireland
ST & LA	Socialist Trade and Labor Alliance

Introduction

James Connolly (1868-1916), is known as Ireland's foremost marxist teacher and activist; the mass working-class leader who effected a union of socialist and nationalist forces in a radical anti-imperialist front after the outbreak of the first world war, and who suffered execution in May 1916 for his prime role in the republican insurrection of Easter week that year. His significance beyond the purely Irish context is less well known. He was a marxist theoretician of major importance and was undoubtedly among the first rank of revolutionary leaders to emerge from the socialist movement of the Second International.

Connolly's execution brought to a premature close a career of over thirty-five years duration in the social democratic and labour movements in Ireland, Scotland and the USA. He was born in Edinburgh in June 1868, in the city's 'little Ireland' quarter, the third son of an immigrant Irish labourer.[1] After a characteristic series of 'dead-end' menial jobs and a seven-year stint as a regular soldier,[2] the young Connolly returned to his native city in 1890 and it was then that he joined the Scottish Socialist Federation, the local affiliate of the British social democratic body. He spent six years in the Edinburgh movement, during which time he received solid grounding in marxist theory and developed formidable prowess in doctrinal exegesis, public speaking and in the concrete tasks of party organisation and management. The process of determined self-education then begun included gaining some degree of familiarity with foreign languages in order to read marxist classics: he seems to have achieved some knowledge of French and German and, at a later point, even Italian.

Between 1896 and 1902, he was paid organiser for the Irish Socialist Republican Party in Dublin, a body which – under his direction – sought to demonstrate the interdependence of the nationalist and socialist struggles. Modelled on the reformist parliamentary practice of British social democracy, this party later foundered when Connolly attempted to commit its membership wholly to the ultra-sectarian line followed by the American Socialist Labor Party. The 'clear cut' approach formulated for the SLP by its leader Daniel De Leon demanded complete dissociation by socialist bodies (including party and union organisations) from 'class unconscious' (i.e. non-marxist) political labour parties and trade unions. In 1903, Connolly helped found a British SLP but later that year was forced by economic necessity to emigrate to the USA.

From the austere De Leon, Connolly accepted the syndicalist (or, more correctly, industrial unionist) schema for revolutionary proletarian mobilisation, but later parted company with him over the American leader's insistence upon a rigidly determinist position on matters of belief and ethics and over De Leon's desire to subordinate the socialist union organisation to party control. Connolly then became an organiser both for the syndicalist Industrial Workers of the World organisation and the reformist Socialist Party of America. and subsequently urged a policy of joint party/union co-operation upon the two bodies. This policy of political-*cum*-industrial strategy remained the basis of Connolly's efforts when he returned to Ireland in 1910. It was then applied both to the working-class struggle and to the national anti-imperialist struggle for Irish independence. This commitment developed from a political to a military dimension of struggle after the outbreak of world war and issued in his move toward insurrection in Easter week 1916.

As an activist involved in the working-class movement in Ireland and the USA, Connolly devoted much time to theoretical work at various levels. On the issue of the nature of working-class strategy to be followed under maturing capitalism, he developed a sophisticated syndicalist methodology, following De Leon's analytical achievement. On the question of the relation of marxism to Irish nationalism, Connolly argued that – in the age of industrial capitalism and imperialism – it was only through socialism that the working people of Ireland could achieve genuine national independence. Nor was this view limited to an economic or pragmatic standpoint: arguing from an historical perspective and through the medium of historical writing, he attempted to demonstrate that only in a socialist polity could the Irish assert as real norms (i.e. in *social practice*) the values of the ancient Gael and medieval christian from whom they received their tradition of nationhood. Connolly's historiography was argued from the most general level of principle. In addition to providing a marxist history of the Irish past, he was seeking to provide a normative system of values (those of Irish christian and Gaelic tradition) to restore conceptual integrity to a contemporary orthodox marxism which had become totally determinist and scientistic in nature. His 'unorthodoxy' of approach in face of the determinist metaphysic of 'scientific socialism', and his perception of the conceptual need to approach the normative problem, raises his theoretical work to a genuine philosophical level.

I would argue that it is in this philosophical contribution that Connolly's claim to be regarded as a truly major marxist theoretician rests. However, his mode of expression, couched as it was in a phraseology appropriate to the party journals of mass struggle, is often of a pragmatic nature not well suited to philosophical content. Those of empirical mind who may tend to reject such a notion of real content for a straightforward literal reading, might consider the following observation from one of the more subtle and erudite commentators on Connolly's intellect.

> Connolly's Catholicism has perhaps been missed by many people because Connolly carried out his work in the forum of working-class politics and social conflict: but one cannot deny the force of a theologian merely because he does not use theological terminology, write for an audience of fellow theologians or publish his arguments in theological journals.[3]

I would endorse this most penetrating comment with the qualification that Connolly's commitment to argue a devotional principle should be seen in the context of a larger commitment to argue on principle generally – i.e. in a truly philosophical manner.

Looking at Connolly's argument from a general philosophical standpoint helps greatly to resolve the issue of the integrity of his thought. Far too often commentators adopt the simplistic approach of contrasting the 'young' with the 'mature' Connolly, the 'nationalist' with the 'socialist', the 'syndicalist' with the 'marxist', and so on. Such reductionist analyses tend toward a description of Connolly as a disintegrative, schizoid intellect without illuminating the very real problem of his complexity of mind. This complexity – and the attempts to thematise Connolly's thinking in a meaningful and principled way, avoiding artificiality – resulted in a somewhat problematic structure for this study. Chapters 1 and 2 below should be read in *parallel* and not in sequence, for they deal with distinct themes in Connolly's thinking to the point reached about 1913. Chapter 1 deals with Connolly's revolutionary nationalism insofar as it involved the accommodation of marxist science to the national and religious traditions of Ireland. The practice of ancient Gaeldom as he understood it, the christian consciousness of Catholicity, together with the secular tradition of political and economic struggle (the bourgeois parliamentary movement excluded) are assessed in terms of Connolly's perception of each as an element in the historical struggle of labour in Ireland against its own subjection. In chapter 2, the evolution of Connolly's syndicalist method is described from the time of his first contact with the American 'Marxist – De Leonist' doctrine around the turn of the century. The interpretation of this doctrine centres on the opinion that it should be regarded as an organisational method distinct from both the reformist parliamentary approach of the Second International and its successor, the 'Marxism – Leninism' of the Comintern. Whatever the shortcomings of this De Leonist approach, it seems to me to be inadmissable to assess it specifically in the terms of either one of these other traditions, and I have limited myself to comparisons in this respect, and only at points when it seemed instructive to make them. Chapter 3 deals with the ultimate crisis faced by Connolly in 1914–16: the impact of Irish partition and world war demanded a profound re-assessment of Connolly's prior assumptions and method. However the argument focuses on the conviction that *in principle* his standpoint remained consistent. The general philosophical issues involved in supplying a normative system drawn from spiritual sources in Irish tradition as a complement to the scientific determinism of orthodox marxism are examined in chapter 4, together with an analysis of his historiographical enterprise which underpinned the entire project. There follows a concluding 'retrospect' on Connolly's concept of the nature of the 'revolutionary' attempt made in Easter week 1916.

A work of intellectual history cannot capture the nature of the man whose thought and thought-in-action comprise its subject matter, and Connolly the man is not described here. Suffice it to say that I have written this study in the conviction that James Connolly was an important figure in the history of socialism, as of Ireland; a 'great man' by any standards with which that historical description may be applied; and a man from whom we might learn in the depth of his intellectual challenge, his receptivity of mind, his courage, his humour and tranquillity in adversity, and his truly awesome nobility of spirit.

1. The Hibernicisation of Marxism*

As an Irish marxist, James Connolly regarded proletarian class consciousness as the ultimate form of nationalist commitment. Basic to this belief was his notion that the cause of freedom in a subject nation could not advance any faster than that of its most subject class. The corollary also held true: that only through an emancipation of its most subject class could a dependent nation achieve genuine autonomy. Hence, the causes of Irish freedom and of Irish labour were coeval.

Such logic, which regarded marxist theory as primarily a revolutionary tool for the use of an anti-imperialist proletarian thrust, is familiar enough. The 'proletarian' nature of the national struggles of colonised peoples against world capitalism has been recognised successively by marxists of the Leninist, Maoist and, most recently, Cuban schools. As it emerged as the faith of the organised working class in late nineteenth century industrial Europe and North America, 'marxism' centred itself on the problem of replacing the established bourgeois political economy with its socialist antithesis. In the dependent territories of the capitalist empires, then as in the twentieth century, marxist strategy could not be resolved into such matters of empirical judgment and calculation. The burden of history is a prime legacy of long-standing imperial relationships, both in terms of the self-definition of the ruled and the perceptions of the rulers. Marxists, like Connolly, from dependent nations were primarily

*An appellation culled by analogy with Mao tse-Tung's notion of the 'Sinification of Marxism': *On the New Stage* (October 1938), quoted Stuart R. Schram, *The Political Thought of Mao tse-Tung,* Harmondsworth, Pelican Books 1969, p.171 ff. Some discussion of Mao and Connolly's shared commitment to accommodate marxist science with nationalist/cultural realities is contained in the introduction to Owen Dudley Edwards and Bernard Ransom eds., *James Connolly – Selected Political Writings* London, Cape 1973.

obliged to articulate their doctrine as a standpoint within the history of the national struggle.

Hence Connolly's task in Ireland centred upon a justification and thorough application of historical materialist method within the Hibernian context, rather than upon arguing the 'economic case' for socialism as his metropolitan British comrades did. Such an 'Hibernicisation' of marxism entailed a programmatic attempt at a detailed accommodation of marxist science to the national and religious traditions of Ireland. In addition to the cultural demands of the Irish context, this historiographical enterprise was necessitated by philosophical considerations of the most general kind, relative to the nature of marxist materialism: these problems will be examined in a later chapter.

The cultural and historical elements of which Connolly had to take account were of two kinds: the ethical values of the pagan Gael and Irish christian, and the achievements (or perhaps more properly, the failures) of the centuries-long Irish revolutionary and national struggle. Connolly's revolutionary nationalism drew heavily upon the values of pagan Gaelic humanism and Irish Catholicity. By 'Catholicity' in this context, it should be noted that Connolly did not mean a sectarian standpoint, but rather a strictly non-denominational corpus of original christian values. These values he regarded as having been denied and eclipsed through seven centuries of Irish history by the proprietorial rights of conquest exercised in the country by the English overlords of the Ascendancy. Connolly believed that the 'reconquest' of Ireland by the Irish people themselves – together with the restoration of Gaelic and christian ethical norms in social practice – would be accomplished in his own lifetime. The instrument of the reconquest would be the Irish working class, educated to its historic task through scientific (marxist) analysis of Irish conditions and history.

The socialist reconquest of Ireland, in addition to bringing about a regeneration of the Gaelic and christian ideals, would also bring to a close the centuries-long Irish revolutionary and national struggle. In this connection, Connolly viewed the modern socialist movement as the successor to all the organisations which had fought in the past for economic and political freedom in Ireland. Among these he numbered popular agrarian movements, undercover insurrectionary groups dedicated to the establishment of an Irish republic through armed struggle and constitutional nationalist political parties. Both in his sustained historical writing and in more programmatic propagandist statements, Connolly emphasised that the socialist revolution would be the ultimate stage in this multi-dimensional Irish revolutionary tradition. Bourgeois constitutional nationalism was of crucial importance: not only was it a vital tradition, but also a potent concrete political force in Connolly's own day, and one which enjoyed the allegiance of the mass of the Irish working people. It was socialism's greatest political rival and posed Connolly the challenge to demonstrate that only socialism could bring its work to a full, non-contradictory conclusion. Accordingly, Connolly set out to show how Irish constitutional leaders, particularly his parliamentarian contemporary John Redmond MP, held concepts of political and social freedom limited to a gentry/middle-class perspective. From this premise he argued that *their* ideal of a free Irish nation could only be given *real* content (i.e. a radical popular nature) in the practice of Irish social democracy.

Connolly first came to work in the Irish movement in May 1896, having been appointed, at the age of 28, full-time organiser of the diminutive Dublin Socialist Society. Dublin socialists, concerned about the relative ineffectiveness of British-produced literature among a working class imbued with Irish nationalist sentiment, had sought out an able propagandist with the ability to create a marxist campaign with a specific Irish standpoint.[1] Connolly came to Dublin with an outstanding reputation as teacher, public speaker and organiser for the socialist movement in his native city.[2] If the whole *raison d'être* for his Dublin appointment was the task of working out a theoretical accommodation between marxist science and the Irish national tradition, it is worth setting out his own standpoint at the time. Connolly at 28 was a committed marxist and an exceptional exponent of the materialist doctrines of 'scientific socialism' as then understood. The point is that he could not then be considered a nationalist: his Edinburgh Irish background had certainly given him a definite *ethnic* consciousness, but this should not be confused or conflated with nationalism as an intellectual/spiritual commitment. Indeed, his total detachment from the emigré Irish nationalist cause in his Edinburgh years is indicated by his municipal campaigns in 1894 and 1895, when his avowed socialist candidacies were advanced in 'Little Ireland' in the teeth of virulent opposition from the local caucus of the Irish National League. It is likely then, that Connolly approached his new task in Dublin primarily with the needs of socialist propaganda and organisation in the Irish context in mind: he was not seeking at that time to give expression to supposedly long-standing 'advanced nationalist' views.[3] However, the orientation of his new comrades in the Dublin Socialist Society could certainly be properly described as 'advanced nationalist'.

As a marxist trained in the Scottish echelons of the British Social Democratic Federation, Connolly brought to the Dublin group the typical democratic-reformist approach of the Second International parties. When, within a few months of his arrival in Dublin, he wrote a new political programme for the local group, it emerged as strongly reformist in tone and greatly indebted to the programme of the British SDF. It spoke of its ultimate goal as '. . .public ownership by the Irish people of the land and instruments of production, distribution and exchange' and of a whole range of reformist measures designed to lead up to this end which would be pressed by socialist representatives on all public bodies in Ireland and in the British House of Commons. Among the immediate reforms advocated were such items as railway and canal nationalisation; the institution of state banks 'issuing loans at cost'; a graduated income tax; state pensions for the aged, widowed and infirm; a 48-hour working week with an established minimum wage, free education and universal suffrage.[4] This was revolution by political evolution; proletarian emancipation by piecemeal reforms enacted by a legislature controlled by workers' representatives. As a programme for the democratic execution of the revolutionary marxist critique of bourgeois society and capitalist property relations, this kind of scenario remained the ruling orthodoxy within the Second International parties.

However, having deliberately stressed the 'orthodoxy' of Connolly's basic approach, it is perhaps easier to delineate how this approach was crucially modified by the 'advanced nationalist' demands of the Irish context. It should now be mentioned that the group for which Connolly drafted this new programme he himself re-named the Irish Socialist Republican Party, dedicated to the complete separation of Ireland from the political structure of the British empire, and the establishment of an Irish socialist republic therein. At the time, the very concept of a 'socialist republic' was a radical and startling one, yet it was the only logical end which could encompass the revolutionary standpoints both of marxism and of Irish nationalism. This new standpoint also demonstrated a necessary logical goal beyond the limited aspirations of Irish Liberalism (i.e. Home Rule constitutionalism) and in so doing set the tone for Connolly's sustained future work to isolate the Home Rule Liberal forces as a political minority beleaguered by an alliance of class-conscious workers and 'uncompromising nationalists'. The concept of that alliance which made possible the heroic *putsch* of Easter 1916, was already evident in Connolly's changed standpoint of 1896.

Connolly adumbrated his new standpoint in a series of articles entitled 'Ireland for the Irish' published in the British Labour newspaper the *Labour Leader* during October 1896 and published by the ISRP the following year as the first edition of his famous booklet *Erin's Hope*. In essence a tract against Home Rule as conceived by Irish Liberals, *Erin's Hope* speaks of the 'earnest Irish worker' joining forces with the 'uncompromising Nationalist in seeking from the advocate of an Irish Socialist Republic the clue of the labyrinthine puzzle of modern economic conditions'.[5] Connolly presented a sustained analysis of the industrial and agricultural aspects of the economic 'labyrinth' in exemplary orthodox style. Arguing from assumptions basic to orthodox marxism's critique of international capitalism, he demonstrated how periodic crises of overproduction and underconsumption were pathological to the system; how competition both in industrial manufacture and in agricultural production had produced mammoth corporate enterprises ever seeking to enlarge their share of 'shrinking' world markets; and how rapid industrialisation in countries such as China and Japan both challenged the manufacturing supremacy of the older established industrial powers like Britain and the USA and disabled potential industrial producers, such as Ireland under Home Rule, from ever achieving 'take-off' point.[6] Connolly was saying nothing new here. It was on the basis of such a 'scientific' prediction of the impending systematic collapse of international capitalism – reiterated time and again by Engels himself and by leading Second International ideologues like Karl Kautsky – that European and North American social democrats confidently anticipated a working-class revolution as a logically predetermined event.

Given this scenario, Connolly argued that Home Rule was reactionary nonsense. In a passage reminiscent of Marx's own discussion of the 'national class' issue in the *Communist Manifesto*, Connolly addressed himself to the ways in which the Irish bourgeoisie sought – through Home Rule – to achieve the necessary legislative licence for a thorough commercial and industrial exploitation of the Irish working class; and to buttress its political and economic grip on the nation further with a large scale extension of individual peasant ownership in agriculture. Marx had described how the bourgeoisie – by virtue of its control of capital – had made successive political advances as industrial manufacture increasingly dominated the late medieval and modern economies: this class now enjoyed exclusive political sway according to Marx, to the point where '. . . the executive of the modern state is but a committee for managing the common affairs of the whole bourgeoisie'.[7] Home Rule, despite assuring a similar dominant position for Irish capitalists, would in no way avert the inevitable disaster which awaited the Irish nation if it sought to challenge the industrial giants on the already glutted world market. Undercapitalised and inexperienced, Ireland's only hope of sustaining sales of its manufactured exports would depend – according to Connolly – '. . . upon our ability to work longer and harder for a lower wage than the other nations of Europe . . . our chance of making Ireland a manufacturing country depends upon us becoming the lowest blacklegs in Europe'.[8]

In order to abort the flowering of this proprietorial horror in Ireland, Connolly was clear that the political evolution of the country would have to bypass the bourgeois-liberal form of the state. Indeed, the objective conditions of the world economy in the age of competing imperialisms amply demonstrated that there was no room for a self-supporting liberal Irish state. Political independence from the British empire could only come about progressively on socialist terms, with both agricultural and industrial production undertaken for community use rather than class profit, by a socialist republican government.[9] This commitment to resist by all possible means the creation of a native liberal polity in Ireland remained a cardinal feature of Connolly's thinking for the remainder of his life. A function of a distinct interpretation of the implications of Irish 'backwardness', it was also a commitment which set him a world apart from mainstream British socialism whose ideologues believed – in true determinist fashion – that Home Rule was at least 'progressive'.[10]

With the mention of this theoretical gulf, we should now consider a radical element apparent in *Erin's Hope* which is of an entirely different logical order from the empirical science of orthodox marxism. The British marxist belief that Home Rule for Ireland (and for every part of the empire) was a necessary 'liberal' phase which must historically precede and prepare the ground for a general working-class upsurge in Britain and its overseas possessions, ran counter to the whole logic of Connolly's approach to contemporary global developments and to the problem of Irish 'backwardness'. This empirical disagreement apart, it has to be observed that Connolly's new notion of a radical nationalist–socialist alliance in Ireland could only be conceived at the expense of jettisoning much of the determinist content of historical materialism as interpreted by the orthodox. It is worth quoting in some detail Connolly's statement of his divergence from orthodox materialist method. Discussing the persistence of 'primitive' communal forms of land tenure in Irish society until well into the seventeenth century, Connolly draws a telling distinction between the approach of what he calls 'the ardent [i.e. determinist-scientific] student of sociology' and 'the sympathetic student of history'.

> The ardent student of sociology, who believes that the progress of the human race through the various economic stages of communism, chattel slavery, feudalism and wage-slavery, has been but a preparation for the higher ordered

> society of the future . . . will perhaps regard the Irish adherence to clan ownership at such a comparatively recent date as the seventeenth century as an evidence of retarded economical development and therefore a real hindrance to progress. But the sympathetic student of history, who believes in the possibility of a people by political intuition anticipating the lessons afterwards revealed to them in the sad school of experience, will not be indisposed to join with the ardent Irish patriot in his lavish expressions of admiration for the sagacity of his Celtic forefathers, who foreshadowed in the democratic organisation of the Irish clan the more perfect organisation of the free society of the future.[11]

For Connolly, working in the late nineteenth century Irish context, a standpoint beyond the orthodox analysis seemed imperative in order to take adequate account of the history of Irish national *consciousness* itself. In *Erin's Hope* he referred to the development of this consciousness from the idea of the 'tribal association' – destroyed by English conquest in the seventeenth century – to that of '. . . the fuller and broader conception of an Irish nation as the natural repository and guardian of the people's heritage'.[12] This 'fuller and broader conception' of nationhood would of course reach its ultimate fulfilment in the established notion of a socialist republic. The historical development of nationalist consciousness, of the *idea* of Irish nationhood, is central to the more sustained treatment given in *Labour in Irish History*: however, even in the seminal argumentation of *Erin's Hope*, the 'historicity' of the concept of nationhood is clearly presented.

At this stage, the immediate purpose of this methodology was to serve a distinct nationalist end. It enabled Connolly to present Home Rule as an *inadequate, historically outmoded conception* of nationalist ideals. Against the historical experience of the nation – wherein until the seventeenth century common ownership of land '. . . formed part of the well defined social organisation of a nation of scholars and students, recognised by Chief and Tanist, Brehon and Bard, as the inspiring principle of their collective life, and the basis of their national system of jurisprudence'[13] – the Irish middle class could advocate only an alien notion of individual proprietorship, learned from their English overlords. Irish industrial and agricultural proprietors Connolly regarded as the ultimate apostates to the national cause. This class he declared:

> . . . while professedly ultra-nationalistic in its political aims, had nevertheless so far compounded with the enemy as to accept the alien social system, with its accompanying manifestations, the legal dispossession and economic dependence of the vast mass of the Irish people as part of the natural order of society.[14]

The Irish middle class owed its position in the nationalist movement of the modern period to a contradictory situation. While their wealth had been derived from the success with which they had found for themselves a niche in the commercial system of the 'Saxon enemy', they derived their political influence from a merely formal adherence to the nationalist cause. They could not support any complete form of national independence, Connolly argued, simply because this would dissolve their economic power base.

For Connolly then, the Irish bourgeoisie, with its economic commitment to alien (English) capitalist property relations, could in principle never lead the national movement beyond a strictly limited form of 'devolved' local self-government within the imperial structure. This standpoint – which reached its ultimate success with the emergence of Gladstone's Home Rule Bills of 1886 and 1893 – he held to be the *antithesis* of the historical struggle of the Irish toward a regeneration of their national freedom. The very limited nature of these measures testified to what economic conditions in the age of imperialism confirmed: mere political reform could never achieve real national goals, nor would they ever be achieved under bourgeois leadership with its limited aspirations.

In Connolly's view it was the fatal effect of this same factor – the impact of a compromising and apostate bourgeois leadership – which led to the ruin of the two chief movements in the Irish nationalist tradition whose legacies the modern socialist party worked to uphold: the insurrectionist United Irishmen and the Land League. From the standpoint of historic logic, Connolly argued, the class principle embodied in the practice of the socialist party would enable it to supply a non-contradictory type of leadership for the Irish revolution in the industrial age. In an Ireland in which religious conflict approached endemic anarchy, the 1798 rebellion attempted by the secular revolutionaries of the United Irishmen was crushed by Irish Protestant yeomanry and aristocratic Catholic militia forces. At the local level the rebel forces were variously Catholic or Presbyterian, being opposed by loyalists generally of the opposite denomination. Irish 'patriot' leaders of the constitutionalist stamp, notably the Whig Henry Grattan and the 'Liberator' Daniel O'Connell, condemned and fought the rebels as dangerous malcontents infected with the levelling doctrines of Republican France. Connolly explicitly made common cause with the internationalism of the United Irish leader Wolfe Tone and with his resolute struggle against bourgeois patriots who sided with British authority against their radical countrymen. Writing on the centenary of the rebellion, Connolly observed,

> Wolfe Tone . . . was crucified in life, now he is idolised in death and the men who push forward most arrogantly to burn incense at the altar of his fame are drawn from the very class who, were he alive today, would hasten to repudiate him as a dangerous malcontent . . . Wolfe Tone was abreast of the revolutionary thought of his day, as are the Socialist Republicans of our day. He saw clearly, as we see, that a dominion as long rooted in any country as British dominion in Ireland can only be dislodged by a revolutionary impulse in line with the development of the entire epoch.[15]

For Connolly, the Irish Land League of 1879-81 was a model of class-conscious action and class struggle. Its leader, Michael Davitt, became committed to the principle of land nationalisation, but, meeting severe resistance to the idea from his allies in Parnell's socially conservative Home Rule party did not press the issue. The League remained formally committed to the petty-bourgeois ideal of peasant ownership and agitated for this reform by means of rent strikes, boycott action and other devices of 'agrarian crime'. Successive Gladstonian Land Acts eventually conceded such reforms, thus vitiating – in Connolly's view – the real potential of the movement for radical collective social and economic change. In an editorial in his American paper *The Harp* in August 1908, Connolly deplored the temerity and ingenuousness of Davitt's leadership. Davitt, he opined, 'gave his name and his services freely at the beck and call of men who despised his ideals'. The lesson of the League's strength in its positive aspects, however,

> . . . lay in the fact that its representatives were the servants and mouthpieces of a class who were already organised and holding the means of production with revolutionary intent . . . Socialist agitators of today . . . must do as the Land League did – take hold of the daily fight in the workshop, and organise it in a revolutionary manner, with a revolutionary purpose and direction.

On a more straightforward political plane, Connolly and the ISRP took a leading part in the nationalist demonstrations staged in June 1897 to counter official ceremonies marking the Diamond Jubilee of Queen Victoria. Anti-monarchist riots in Dublin and other Irish centres that month served notice of a widespread popular disaffection in the country, despite official displays designed to demonstrate Ireland's loyalty. At this time, the socialist republicans first achieved a sustained co-operation with radical nationalists from the literary and cultural movement: these included Alice Milligan of Belfast, Maude Gonne (with the young Yeats in train) and others from the *ad hoc* committees which had sprung up to organise a commemoration of the United Irish rebellion of 1798. The Transvaal crisis of 1899 and the resultant hostilities between British and Boer forces in South Africa came as a further occasion for socialist and nationalist co-operation in a joint anti-imperialist protest. From the outset, Connolly took a determined pro-Boer stand on internationalist lines, substantially similar to his own and Lenin's 'revolutionary defeatist' approach in the later world war crisis of 1914. The ISRP became a leading element in the Irish Transvaal Committee, an *ad hoc* collection of nationalists of all shades united to oppose Ireland's participation in the war. Writing in his

Workers' Republic on 19 August, Connolly drew attention to some implications for revolutionary practice of the British war upon the Boer republics:

> We do not like to theorise upon the function of force as a midwife to progress, that . . . is a matter to be settled by the enemies of progress – but we cannot afford to remain blind to the signs of the time. If then, we see a small section of the possessing class prepared to launch two nations into war, to shed oceans of blood and to spend millions of treasure, in order to maintain intact a *small portion* of their privileges, how can we expect the entire propertied class to abstain from using the same weapons, and to submit peacefully when called upon to *yield up forever all their privileges?* Let the working class democracy of Ireland note that lesson and, whilst working peacefully while they may, keep constantly before their minds the truth that the capitalist class is a beast of prey and cannot be moralised, converted, or conciliated, but must be extirpated.

This vision of the possible use of force by the workers in the socialist revolution in circumstances of war, or as the ultimate recourse, is an important precedent* for Connolly's standpoint in 1916. Meanwhile, so effective was the peaceful anti-war campaign mounted by the ISRP and its allies, that – despite substantial unemployment in the country and a whirlwind Irish tour by the Queen herself – the recruiting effort for the British forces languished.

There was little in the way of concrete results from this co-operation, partly because the South African war was itself drawing to a close in 1900 and partly as a result of a reunification of nationalist parliamentary forces in the same year. After almost a decade of factionalism which succeeded Parnell's death in 1891, Home Rule constitutionalists reformed into a new United Irish League under the leadership of John Redmond MP. This reorganisation ensured that Irish Liberals would not lose

*According to one account, Arthur Griffith recalled that Connolly suggested to him at this time the idea that certain strongpoints in Dublin might be held and fortified and an Irish republic proclaimed. See Maureen Wall, 'The Background to the Rising' in K. Nowlan ed., *The Making of 1916*, Dublin, Stationery Office 1969, p.190, note 15.

leadership to the more fragmented radical nationalists. There was also the question of the *kind* of propaganda which the radical groups were capable of. Connolly's comments on some of the political weaknesses of his allies at this time are very instructive:

> . . . These agencies, whether Irish Language movements, Literary societies or Commemoration Committees, are undoubtedly doing a work of lasting benefit to this country in helping to save from extinction the precious racial and national history, language and characteristics of our people.
>
> Nevertheless, there is a danger that by too strict an adherence to their present methods of propaganda, and consequent neglect of vital living issues, they may only succeed in stereotyping our historical studies into a worship of the past, or crystallising nationalism into a tradition – glorious and heroic indeed, but still only a tradition.[16]

In other words – according to Connolly – the nationalism of the Irish cultural renaissance lacked real programmatic content. It was indeed inferior in this regard to that of the Liberal parliamentarians, who offered self-government within the empire and the chimera of a 'progressive' industrialised Ireland.

This brings us to a crucial point. Such a 'crystallised' nationalism, depending upon 'glorious and heroic' tradition, was above all else *abstract* in nature and easily reducible to mere sentiment. As a vague but impelling call to action this abstract sentiment had motivated the romantic intellects of the 'Young Ireland' revolutionists of 1848: it had no less an impact on the '. . . more diffuse romanticism . . .'[17] of Connolly's own generation. To this abstraction, Connolly sought to give a material content in the form of a socialist programme suited to Irish conditions. As we have seen, this involved an economic regime of the strictest autarky in both agriculture and industry, with production for *social* use being organised by a socialist republican government. Connolly's reading of the peculiar implications of Irish 'backwardness' had convinced him of the need to bypass the liberal state form in a direct revolutionary act utilising the class-conscious workers' ballot. The orthodox means to effect this unorthodox end remained the democratic-parliamentary process, and comprised Connolly's own 'permanent revolution' strategy.

In Connolly's theoretical work, the fusion of romanticism with marxism is marked by such features as the idealisation of the traditional Irish septal system and its communal land tenure without reference either to the human slavery basic to it or to the problem of how far an aggregate of tribal units could ever be considered a 'nation' in the true modern (post-feudal) sense of the term. Both of these issues are either side-stepped or ignored in *Erin's Hope* and in *Labour in Irish History*. Indeed, at no time did Connolly follow Marx's example and apply himself to a sustained logical analysis of such pre-capitalist economic relations as were involved in the collective tribal unit. Nor would such an academic effort have endeared him to those nationalist romantics with whom he wished to co-operate. *The* analysis he wished them to accept – in 1900 as in 1916 – was that in the age of imperialism, Ireland had to be socialist as well as sovereign and independent, in order to achieve true national freedom. Like them, Connolly looked to the Gaelic past for *inspiration*: he found it not as they did simply in the heroic acts of a cultivated people, but in that people's adherence to values inimical to those of latter day capitalism.

If the economic and social life of the ancient Gael had developed in Ireland an enduring sense of collective values, the religious observance of his medieval descendants had contributed universal christian values which remained fundamental to the modern Irish consciousness. In his own lifetime – regarded by him as the period of maturing international capitalism – Connolly argued that only under a socialist order could these values again become actualised in social practice.

The key to Connolly's standpoint in the matter is again his concern for the historical development of Irish consciousness. He regarded Irish adherence to Catholicity – especially during the period of intense political and religious persecution in the seventeenth and eighteenth centuries – as more than an episode in church history or religious development. He saw it as an important moment in the development of a unique Irish consciousness, of the *idea* of Irish nationality. To be specific, Connolly stressed the importance of Catholicity as a value system opposed to the

Protestant ethic of Ireland's English overlords and to the nascent ideals of capitalism implicit in the Protestant Reformation itself. The post-medieval religious distinction between English and Irish values overlaid the more ancient one in matters of political economy: English Protestantism clashed with Irish Catholicism in the same way as English feudatories confronted Irish septs in an earlier age. Connolly had a very developed – one might say very Catholic – notion of the parameters of spiritual and temporal authority. He had no doubt that – particularly in the Irish context – the church could ask for no better Caesar than the socialist type with whom to co-exist as it pursued its own spiritual mission.

This distinction between the domain of the spiritual and the temporal is a prime indication of Connolly's own rootedness in the Catholic tradition, and underlay the ISRP's commitment to the secularist-humanist line of the Second International on the religious issue. This approach – adopted by the German Social Democratic Party at its congress at Erfurt in 1891 – declared religion to be a private matter, outside the scope of party pronouncement. Referring to this humanist line, Connolly wrote:

> . . . we feel that socialism is based upon a series of facts requiring only unassisted human reason to grasp and master all their details, whereas religion of every kind is admittedly based upon 'faith' in the occurrence in past ages of a series of phenomena inexplicable by any process of mere human reasoning . . . Socialism . . . is neither free-thinker nor Christian, Turk nor Jew, Buddhist nor idolator, Mohammedan nor Parsee – it is only HUMAN.[18]

Yet, by 'human', Connolly did not mean that socialism could be reduced to a straightforward secularist standpoint. Such an assumption was axiomatic among socialists in the English-speaking world generally: straightforward materialists basically assumed that – after the proletarian revolution – religious belief and all other kinds of 'irrationalism' and 'superstitions' would share the fate of the bourgeois state and wither. This kind of materialist totalitarianism was completely foreign to Connolly's temperament, so much so that he could foresee the probability of the church's positive support of socialist doctrine as its political advance progressed. Indeed, in the context of the Irish national struggle, Connolly pointed out that the church's *post hoc* blessing of successive phases within it amounted to a positive intellectual-spiritual contribution to it. Sensitive to the persistent tension within the church between the hierarchy's *modus vivendi* with the political powers that be and lowly priests who regularly spoke out against political and social oppressors, he anticipated a future support for Irish socialism from this quarter:

> . . . the Catholic Church always accepts the established order, even if it has warred on those who have striven to establish such order . . . in Ireland the Church denounced every Irish revolutionary movement in its day of activity, as in 1798, 1848 and 1867, and yet allowed its priests to deliver speeches in eulogy of the active spirits of those movements a generation afterwards, [and] . . . in the future the Church, which has its hand close upon the pulse of human society, when it realises the cause of capitalism is a lost cause, it will find excuse enough to allow freedom of speech and expression to those lowly priests whose socialist declarations it will then use to hide the absolute anti-socialism of the Roman propaganda . . .[19]

In other words, despite definitively anti-socialist declarations from the Vatican such as the papal encyclical 'De Rerum Novarum' of 1891, socialism in Ireland – as a logical extension of revolutionary nationalism – might look to the church for powerful and influential allies.

Connolly spelled out his understanding of the spiritual-temporal distinction in a rejoinder to a Jesuit critic penned in November 1912:

> For the greater part of seven centuries, the *de facto* government of Ireland has been a foreign government imposed upon the country by force and maintained by the same means. The Holy See was compelled by its position to recognise that government, but the holiest and deepest feelings of the Catholics of Ireland were in rebellion against that government, and in every generation the scaffold and

the prison and the martyr's grave have been filled in Ireland with devout subjects of the Holy See, but unrelenting enemies of the *de facto* government of Ireland.

The firm distinction in the minds of Irish Catholics between the *duties* of the Holy See and the *rights* of individual Catholics has been a necessary and saving element in keeping Ireland Catholic . . .[20]

For Connolly, the adherence of the Irish to Roman Catholicism – especially in the teeth of the extremities of legal, social and political persecution practised by the Protestant ascendancy in the seventeenth and eighteenth centuries – was comparable to the stand of the 'slaves and labourers' of ancient Rome who formed the earliest christian congregations. In each case, he suggests, the 'holiest and deepest feelings' of christian people led them to take a collective stand against bondage and oppression.[21] The important point to grasp from all of this is that – from Connolly's perspective at least – Catholicism involved no adjustment between ultimate values and practice in terms of an ideological compromise with temporal needs. Such an ideological pragmatism was indeed basic to the Protestant standpoint with its erastian notions of church government and emphasis upon the individual's obligation to earn self-salvation in the here-and-now. Pragmatism did exist within Catholicism, but only as a *political* stand forced upon the Holy See and the hierarchy by constitutional and diplomatic realities. Such a tradition of an accommodation of *convenience* (as opposed to one of *principle*) between the Roman Catholic church and Protestant powers had, in Connolly's view, facilitated a kind of ethical alienation among Irish Catholics from the *de facto* English rule in Ireland. In other words it had fostered Irish nationalism, despite all formal attempts on the part of the Irish hierarchy to preach social and political acquiescence in the terms of the Conquest. Connolly always showed a readiness to make this point in blunt and colourful imagery:

Well, it is like this. In Ireland all the Protestants are Orangemen and howling Jingoes. If the children go to the Protestant schools they get taught to wave the Union Jack and worship the English King. If they go to the Catholic

Church they become rebels. Which would you sooner have?[22]

The revolutionary implications of Irish Catholicism were of course eccentric elements in the general European political perspective, as Connolly pointed out with some irony:

> . . . Catholicism, which in most parts of Europe is synonymous with Toryism, lickspittle loyalty, servile worship of aristocracy and hatred of all that savours of genuine political independence on the part of the lower classes, in Ireland is almost synonymous with rebellious tendencies, zeal for democracy, and intense feeling of solidarity with all strivings upwards of those who toil . . . the Protestant elements of Ireland were, in the main, a plantation of strangers upon the soil from which the owners had been dispossessed by force. This economic dispossession was, perforce, accompanied by a political and social outlawry. Hence, every attempt of the dispossessed to attain citizenship, to emerge from their state of outlawry, was easily represented as a tentative step towards replanting the Catholic and dispossessing the Protestant.[23]

Connolly regarded the democratic franchise – even as exercised under an attenuated Home Rule constitution – as the ultimate vehicle for the achievement of true national liberty. Or, to be more precise, he did so before the eruption of the joint partition and world war crises in 1914. For the purpose of the present argument, the most important point is that he conceptualised the end of revolutionary Catholicism, newly equipped with 'numerical voting power', as a general spiritual liberation for Catholic and Protestant alike. True, Irish Protestantism would lose its privileged position in social and political life; but – in Connolly's view – this gross and unnatural situation would be replaced with ' . . . the possibilities of an immense spiritual uplifting; an emergence into a knowledge of its kinship with its brothers and sisters of different creeds'.[24] This view co-existed in Connolly's mind with the, perhaps oversanguine, assumption that Irish Catholics had learned over the centuries to generalise their revolt to the level of principle beyond the standpoint of mere sectarianism. He averred:

> Just as the socialist knows that the working class, being the lowest in the social system, cannot emancipate itself without as a result emancipating all other classes, so the Irish Catholic has realised that he, being the most oppressed and disfranchised, could not win any modicum of political freedom or social recognition for himself without winning it for all others in Ireland . . . He has learned that his struggle is, and has been, the struggle of all the lowly and dispossessed, and he has grown broadminded with the broadmindedness of the slave in revolt against slavery.[25]

It was Connolly's view that the principled standpoint beyond sectarianism necessary for the revolutionary Catholic tradition in the twentieth century, was that of marxist socialism. And it was socialism alone, he averred, which could provide a serious principled foundation for a secular state in Ireland. As such, a socialist republic would be the first polity in Irish history freed from the prime duty of applying religious sanctions upon a distrusted population in the interests of England's national security. During the years of his second period of activity in Ireland (1910–16), Connolly's propaganda was directed toward convincing the common Irishman that, *as a wage-worker*, his interests were best served by the socialist party struggling for the establishment of a genuinely secular state dedicated to economic and social emancipation: a state which would allow and demand spiritual freedom for all of its citizens to practise the religious observance of their choice. Now this approach ran into heavy opposition of what might fairly be termed a 'theocratic' nature from both Catholic and Protestant establishments in Ireland. Very broadly, Connolly's notion of the socialist state as a material co-worker with the missionary (Catholic) church clashed with the hierarchy's will to secure political safeguards for Catholic values in Ireland and with its traditional fears of 'Jacobinism' – red terror and godless revolutionary chaos.[26] On the other hand, Ulster Protestantism, with its principled commitment to the post-Reformation British state feared papist domination in any proposed all-Ireland polity, no matter how secular in conception.

So strong were these theocratic alternatives that they would determine the character of politics in Ireland from the time of Connolly's death to that of our own day. Scandalised by the sordidness of the Parnell Divorce, yet fearful of the implications of militant socialism and trade unionism, the Catholic hierarchy swung its support to militant nationalism in the decade preceding the first world war: eventually the constitution of the Irish Republic accorded it a special recognition and protection.[27] In Ulster, the Protestant establishment cemented its union with Britain through Partition, and in 1921 received its own local erastian political structure with the opening of the 'Protestant Parliament for a Protestant People', governing the separate state of Northern Ireland.

This glimpse of future events is useful for the present argument insofar as it shows the magnitude of the task Connolly had set himself. After his return to Ireland in 1910, he evolved an integrated scheme of political-*cum*-industrial revolutionary struggle which might be described as the Irish democratic road to socialism. The Socialist Party of Ireland, of which Connolly became national organiser, was to be assisted in its task of political propaganda by a national industrial union, the Irish Transport Workers' Union. The ITWU – of which Connolly became Belfast secretary in June 1911 – was a syndicalist body dedicated both to organising the workers for the ultimate revolutionary act of an industrial expropriation of the capitalist class and to providing, in its own structure, the administrative fabric which would succeed the bourgeois state. For Connolly, the syndicalist union was the prime vehicle for the national and economic struggle of the Irish working class.(See chapter 2 below.) With these class-conscious party and union structures forcing the pace, he envisaged that the general labour movement in Ireland would evolve toward a revolutionary standpoint beyond conventional trade union bargaining and parliamentary politics. A third element in Connolly's revolutionary coalition was the Irish Labour Party – formed at his suggestion by the Irish TUC in 1912 – as the electoral arm of organised labour in the country. The Labour Party was designed to operate under the new constitution to be established by the Third Home Rule Bill, scheduled to have its first reading in the

British House of Commons in April 1912. It would ensure that the working class would have a distinct voice in the new Irish legislature. For Connolly, that voice would be the harbinger of the democratic revolutionary seizure by the Irish working class of the conditions of its own freedom.

Meanwhile, theoretical work was as urgent as that of party and union organisation. Connolly had to address himself to the theocratic challenge both from the Catholic hierarchy and from apologists for the Protestant erastianism of the North: in the latter case, his opponents were to be found within the Northern labour movement itself. As we have seen, neither of these viewpoints could – for radically different reasons – admit the secularism basic to Connolly's approach. It was therefore necessary for him to agitate the principle of the autonomy of the state *per se* in order to assert that of *class autonomy* with all of its implications of proletarian revolution in Ireland. As a marxist working in a twentieth century Ireland which remained moulded in the public forms of the Reformation and Counter-Reformation, his struggle 'telescoped' bourgeois and working-class aims. Such a concept of the revolutionary task under conditions of relative backwardness is a familiar feature of the Marxist-Leninist approach; and, like the Leninists of Russia, Connolly had to grapple with the problem of erecting a genuinely class-conscious workers' movement on the ruins of a failed Liberalism. In Ireland this consisted in arguing the case for a non-theocratic political standpoint against the proponents of Counter-Reformation theocracy and Reformation erastianism.

Connolly's debate with the Catholic hierarchy began even before his actual return to Dublin from the USA in July 1910, and, logically enough it had been the activities of the syndicalist ITWU which had prompted the vehement clerical response to marxist thinking. Formed in 1909 by the fiery and charismatic militant Jim Larkin, the new union had achieved a considerable membership among the demoralised unskilled workers of Dublin: its orientation was both revolutionary socialist and 'advanced nationalist'. (See chapter 2 below.) To the mentality of orthodox Catholicism, the ITWU ideology appeared as:

> An entirely material concept of life, from which every idea

> of God, the soul, moral obligations, and even intelligence was carefully eliminated, was constantly insisted on. A full stomach was put before the people as the one thing in life worth striving for – the next life did not count . . . the worst passions of our nature, and these alone, were appealed to: pride, cupidity and selfishness . . . the upright spiritualised Irishman for the time disappeared, and all of the brute that was in him was drawn out and fed.[28]

It was sentiments such as these which prompted an attempt at an ultimate intellectual death-blow to socialism by clerical authorities in 1910. The Lenten lectures against socialism delivered in that year in Dublin by the Jesuit preacher Father Robert Kane amounted to a sustained and comprehensive indictment, backed by the authority of the leading intellectual cadre of the church in Ireland. Many hundreds would have attended the sermons and tens of thousands would have read of their content in newspapers and in pamphlet reprints. Dublin socialists asked Connolly – then still resident in the USA – urgently to prepare a rebuttal. This resulted in what is perhaps one of Connolly's most successful, subtle and carefully researched polemical works, *Labour, Nationality and Religion*. Perhaps the most important achievement of Connolly's argument in this pamphlet is his success in demonstrating the gulf between Father Kane's assumptions about economic and social matters and the principles of Catholicity in general. Arguing consistently *on the basis of* Catholic principles, Connolly brings out the *relative* nature of Father Kane's assertions and their logical variance from the expressed precepts of selected Fathers and Saints of the early church. Or, to put it another way, he demonstrates the degree to which the official clerical view on such issues had accommodated itself to the basic values of bourgeois society, systematically denying its own principled origins. Connolly is able to show with ease that – at his most superficial – Father Kane is capable of little more than special pleading for conventional bourgeois mores. Quoting Pope Leo XIII's encyclical on labour, Father Kane states:

> The Socialists, working on the poor man's envy of the rich, endeavour to destroy private property, and maintain that

> personal property should become the common property of all. They are emphatically unjust, because they would rob the lawful possessor . . . [29]

He adds two aphorisms as follows: 'Man's right to live is also the right to take the means wherewith to live' *and*, 'His right to use these means is at the same time a right to exclude others from their use'.

Connolly comments:

> That is to say that a man has the right to take the means wherewith to live, and he has also the right to prevent other men taking the means wherewith to live. The one right cancels the other . . . *Capitalism and landlordism are based upon the denial to Man of his right to live except as a dependent upon capitalists and landlords; they exist by perpetually confiscating the property which the worker has in the fruits of his toil, and establish property for the capitalist by denying it to the labourer.*

Having thus exposed the contradictions fundamental to the clerical position, Connolly calls upon the evidence of myriad anti-proprietorial statements from early christian fathers to refute the papal definition of 'christian democracy' as one which maintains ' . . . that the right of acquiring and possessing property cannot be gainsaid [and safeguarding] the various distinctions and degrees which are indispensable in every well-ordered commonwealth'.[30] Connolly's evidence is drawn from statements attributed to figures such as St Clement, St Basil the Great, St Ambrose and St Chrysostom: included are St Ambrose's definition of private property as a form of 'unjust usurpation' and St Chrysostom's striking aphorism 'The rich man is a thief'.[31]

Having dealt with property relations, Connolly takes Father Kane to task over the issue of the latter's notion of a 'providentially' organised structure and a divinely ordained hierarchy. Still arguing from a decidedly *devotional* standpoint, he accuses his opponent of 'rank blasphemy' since, he avers, the cleric is imputing to the hand of God, responsibility for social conditions which are really the reflection of man's worst instincts. At this juncture Connolly reminds his readers that the origin of private property in Ireland was the English conquest of the country in the eleventh century, with its concomitant slaughter and enslavement of thousands of Irish christians.[32] Narrowing his comments to a specifically denominational view, Connolly then attacks Father Kane for his confused and misleading remarks on the social practice of the Protestant and Catholic churches in the past. Kane attempted a comparison between the record of the pre-Reformation church in alleviating poverty, aiding the destitute and in the provision of education and that of the Protestant Tudor monarchy which extirpated the 'sturdy beggars', destitutes who lacked a refuge after the dissolution of the monastic orders. Connolly regards this device as hypocrisy, since the priest is at once denouncing the Protestant Reformation, while vigorously defending the proprietorial rights of the Protestant conquerors of Ireland who were responsible for the introduction of capitalist structures to the country. He protested: 'Now the church curses the Protestant Reformation, the child; and blesses capitalism – its parent!'[33]

These few examples of the kind of logic Connolly employed in this particular debate indicate how – for him – marxism was itself a standpoint committed to the realisation of universal values long embodied in the christian conscience. Indeed, in the age of triumphalist international capitalism and machinofacture, he argued it was the *only* standpoint which offered a programme for their realisation as actual human practice. Since the church, as an official and hierarchic structure, had thus sold the pass to values which were simply relative and codified expressions of bourgeois self-interest, the marxist movement (party and union) would have to take up the cause where the church had failed. Marxist materialism, far from seeking to destroy real values, would, Connolly averred, base its programmes upon them: or as he put it, 'divine discontent and pity' would be gathered and directed by a socialist administration for the cause of 'social righteousness'.[34] Arguing thus from a standpoint *within* Catholicism, Connolly prepared the ground for winning much sympathy among younger romantic Catholic nationalists in the Sinn Fein and Volunteer movements: to many among the more thoughtful of them, the official church approach must have seemed superficially dogmatic and distant from social realities. Most of the 1916 leaders, themselves zealots fired by a near-messianic virtue, had accepted by the end that Connolly's marxism was in its own way an equal expression of those national and Catholic values for which they were ready to make the ultimate sacrifice.* One might add that it also offered a far more coherent and convincingly systematic analysis of both the problems and the possibilities for a realisation of those values under modern economic and social conditions than any which they possessed.

Other elements in *Labour, Nationality and Religion*, such as Connolly's deft rebuttals of Father Kane's rather obvious assaults on historical materialism and the labour theory of value (not of course a peculiarly marxist concept) defended marxist technique from what was at best shallow misrepresentation and at worst a disingenuous attempt to create prejudice. As an event in the intellectual life of the period, this pamphlet served notice on clerical authorities that Irish marxism, no less than Irish nationalism, was deeply imbued with spiritual values and could not be treated as some kind of determinist import from the degenerate world of Anglo-Saxon and continental European secularity.

The promise of Home Rule convinced Connolly and his comrades in the SPI that a unified and distinctive form of socialist organisation and practice appropriate to the emergent Irish polity had become a priority. Now this determination led Connolly on a collision course with the loyalist Labour tradition embodied in the Belfast branches of the British ILP. This loyalist approach, stressing the contiguity of the industrialised North of Ireland with metropolitan Britain, was diametrically opposed to the nativist historiography upon which Connolly had constructed his own Irish socialist schematic – a construct which was itself attuned to and part of the cultural renaissance which then convulsed contemporary 'Catholic' Ireland. With an article entitled 'A Plea for Socialist Unity in Ireland' in the Glasgow socialist journal *Forward* of 27 May 1911, Connolly commenced an unremitting intellectual campaign against the mentality of Ulster erastianism. The article also began his celebrated debate

*Among the signatories of the 1916 Proclamation of the Irish Republic, these included Thomas MacDonagh, Eamonn Ceannt and P. H. Pearse.

with the Belfast ILP leader William Walker in that forum which ended by editorial discretion the following July. William Walker was then in the process of enlarging his political interest and ambitions from the confines of Belfast to the national British orbit. He was a member of the British Labour Party's national executive and, in 1910 had unsuccessfully contested for Labour the Scottish parliamentary seat of Leith Burghs. Earlier in his political career, he had failed three times to win the Ulster seat of Belfast North – in the general election of 1906 and in two by-elections in 1905 and 1907. His platform in those contests showed how little room for manoeuvre any serious Labour candidacy had in loyalist Belfast. Walker unflinchingly presented himself as a Unionist and worse, albeit under pressure, at one point went on record as saying that the causes of Labour and Protestantism were synonymous. After the latter outburst, his 1905 election agent (none other than J. Ramsay MacDonald) was only narrowly persuaded against resignation in disgust.

At the 1911 Irish TUC it had been on Walker's counter-motion that Connolly's proposal for the establishment of a separate Irish Labour Party had been thrown out, and Connolly's still smouldering vexation would become very evident during the *Forward* debate. Also evident is that Connolly's decision to attack Walker personally was directed against his opponent's personal influence within the Northern movement; he suspected him of being further to the right than many Belfast ILPers. Walker's determined unionist stand was not shared by all of his comrades, many of whom later acceped the need for an Irish Labour Party and for a Home Rule constitution. This accommodation remained loyalist in nature – Home Rule was a *loyalist* measure insofar as it was a rejection of the ultimate *separatist/republican* approach. Connolly's Northern strategy was clearly an eventual conversion of these loyalist comrades to the separatist position on the basis of a shared commitment to (and after some experience of) an operating Home Rule constitution. But first, the negative legacy of 'Walkerism' had to be addressed and discredited.

Opening his polemical attack upon Walker's unionist standpoint, Connolly argued the necessity for a concentration and unification of the socialist forces in Ireland with little tenderness in spelling out the terms. He condemned the Belfast

ILP for its intransigent long-standing opposition both to Home Rule and to the very idea of a distinct Irish Labour Party: implicitly he demanded that the Belfast comrades recognise the incorrectness of their attitude on these matters and accept the SPI line as a precondition to the amalgamation of the two organisations. For Connolly, the Belfast attitude was based upon a false conception of internationalism, a misconception which was itself a function of the dues-paying, organic relationship between the Belfast body and its parent British organisation. He wrote:

> The SPI considers itself the only International party in Ireland, since its conception of Internationalism is that of a free federation of free peoples, whereas that of the Belfast branches of the ILP seems scarcely distinguishable from Imperialism, the merging of subjugated peoples in the political system of their conquerors . . . This is a unique conception of Internationalism, unique and peculiar to Belfast. There is no 'most favoured nation clause' in Socialist diplomacy, and we as socialists in Ireland, cannot afford to establish such a precedent.[35]

Connolly bluntly attacked Walker by name as a prime mover in these errors, adding that had he (Walker) been successful in his Ulster parliamentary candidacies such a victory,

> . . . would have killed the hopes of Socialism among Irish nationalists the world over, [while] . . . the conviction spreads throughout Ireland that the rise of the ILP in Belfast means nothing for Social Democracy in Ireland, but is simply the sign of a family quarrel among the Unionists.

It has to be said that Walker's attempts to justify his own position in terms of the advanced 'municipal socialism' of Belfast and with assertions of the value of Protestant contributions to the Irish national cause (contributions which were based upon an approach flatly contradictory to his own) failed to carry conviction. Connolly marshalled formidable support for his own argument on the nationality issue comprising: the known commitment of Marx to Irish self-government, the consistent support for the Irish national cause given by leading figures of the British socialist movement, the authority of the International itself (which recognised the distinct Irish nation at its Paris congress of 1900) and the testimony of renowned publicists of the international socialist movement such as Jean Jaurès and Gabriel Deville.[36] The vitriolic nature of the debate – something rather uncharacteristic of Connolly in his mature years – indicates the depth of the animosity between the two men and their distinct standpoints. The cleavage had many dimensions: the socialist-republican/labour-loyalist rift mirrored economic distinctions between Connolly, an unskilled worker and syndicalist theorist, an official of the Irish TWU and Walker as a skilled tradesman, an official of the Amalgamated Society of Carpenters and Joiners. Questions of the most general theoretical kind were also involved. While Connolly's stand was based upon both the scripture and oral tradition (so to speak) of marxist doctrine, Walker's thinking was of the kind (very widespread in the ILP) which ultimately rejected historical materialism. Having very little real connection with marxism as historical 'science', this ILP approach was at base a restatement of late eighteenth century radical political economy as taught by Adam Smith and David Ricardo: hence the issue of a consistent application of marxist principles to historical problems (such as nationality) did not arise.

In his approach to the Ulster problem, it should be noted that Connolly did not overstress the matter of the uneven development of capitalism in Ireland. No-one could be more aware than he of the divergence between the industrialised economy of Belfast, with its distinct and well organised proletariat, and the relatively underdeveloped Southern economy with its largely rural workforce. However, in his attempt to 'resolve' the differences between the two contexts in terms of the creation of a unified, all-Ireland socialist movement, Connolly relied upon a general acceptance of a 'correctness' of attitude on the national question. This approach demanded – especially of the Ulster comrades – a wholesale abandonment of prior practice based in experience in favour of the argument of abstract theory. This was the kind of appeal that Connolly made to the Northern movement, 'over the head', so to speak, of the reactionary

Walker. In fairness to the very real difficulties Northern socialists might have had with Connolly's overtures, it should be said that these very overtures demanded that they abandon their fears of nationalist capitalism of the *Sinn Fein* variety and such protection from all capitalist exploitation (North and South in Ireland) as their tangible links with British social democracy afforded them, in favour of the 'correct' consciousness possessed by Connolly himself and the diminutive SPI. To some extent, it has to be admitted that the loyalist socialism of Belfast was itself a product of the weakness of socialism in the nationalist movement of the South. Irish nationalism – as Connolly himself had found from his earliest years in Dublin – was generally profoundly anti-labour and anti-socialist: before the turn of the century Connolly's own Socialist Republican Party had lacked the strength to prevail against it even in Southern provincial centres, leave alone achieving an independent impact in Belfast. Connolly's re-appearance on the Irish scene from 1910 onwards – even with his weight of unimpeachable marxist argument on the national issue – was a taxing model to follow for Northern socialists used to viewing Irish nationalism as a nativist doctrine devoid of social content. It was a testament both to Connolly's powers of argumentation and to the Northern comrades' general respect for theory that he made the progress he did for the socialist republican cause in his Belfast years (1911-13).

In 1912, William Walker accepted a government post under the National Insurance Act and went out of the labour movement, but even before his departure, it became clear that Connolly had won substantial support for his position within the Northern movement. On Easter Monday of 1912, the three branches of the SPI, three branches of the Northern ILP (Walker's own North Belfast branch being self-excluded), together with the diminutive Belfast branch of the new British Socialist Party, were all represented at a unity conference convened by Connolly in Dublin. Agreement was reached to unite on the basis of the SPI's position and the new Independent Labour Party of Ireland was inaugurated on an all-Ireland pattern. This agreement involved commitment both to political activity *within* the new self-governing constitution expected to emerge from the enactment of the third Irish Home Rule Bill and to syndicalist method and practice in the industrial field.* However, 'Walkerism' remained strong within the Northern movement, especially as it came under increasing sectarian pressure from Unionist forces seeking to quell all kinds of disaffection which might distract popular attention from the priority of resistance to the Home Rule Bill. Throughout 1912 and 1913, the activities of the local ILP, ILP (I) and the Belfast branch of the ITWU were virtually brought to a standstill by a mounting campaign of Unionist intimidation, harassment and economic proscription. In the midst of this desperate situation Connolly continued his attempts to bring Northern 'Walkerites' into line on the national issue and to slough off their commitment to the Protestant Reformation state. He commented:

> When striving to induce my Belfast comrades to adopt this policy . . . I was asked did I think it would make our propaganda easier. I answered that I did not, that on the contrary it would arouse passions immensely more bitter than had ever been met here by the socialist movement in the past, but it would make our propaganda more fruitful and our organisation more enduring . . .
>
> Therefore we declare to the Orange workers of Belfast that we stand for the right of the people of Ireland to rule as well as to own Ireland, and cannot conceive of a separation of the two ideas; and to all and sundry we announce that as Socialists we are Home Rulers, but that on the day the Home Rule government goes into power, the Socialist movement in Ireland will go into opposition.[37]

Such were the uncompromising terms upon which Connolly offered the decimated and leaderless ILP 'rump' in Belfast his own party's supportive co-operation in these difficult years. By May of 1913, the two organisations had formed a joint managing committee to supervise all future socialist propaganda in the city. It seems clear that, as the political crisis over the Home Rule Bill became more acute, Connolly hoped he might bring about a fusion of the two parties and thus liquidate the last tangible remains of the erastian heterodoxy in the Northern labour

*The programme of the ILP(I) is described in the following chapter.

movement. The ultimate purpose of such a political fusion seems clear from his comment, or rather *promise*, that the reorganised Irish socialist movement would form the opposition in the new Home Rule parliament. Connolly clearly regarded the eventual alignment in the new Irish assembly as between capital (North and South) and socialist labour on an all-Ireland basis. Such a direct parliamentary confrontation between defined capitalist and socialist/labour parties (as opposed to the conventional Conservative – Liberal alignment, each with class-unconscious working-class cohort support) had long been desired by British socialists. Such a direct class confrontation would lead to a final assumption of *legitimate* power by the socialist movement through a democratic, parliamentary *coup d'état*: this political seizure of power would herald the revolutionary restructuring of the economy and society. In Ireland, Connolly anticipated that the two forms of capital – nationalist and unionist – would be obliged to consolidate their forces in the new assembly under their true colours: opposition to them would be given by a unified Irish socialist/labour party, supported by a working class freed from its historical bourgeois unionist and nationalist affiliations and organised industrially in growing, class-conscious syndicalist unions.

Such was Connolly's standpoint in 1913. That year, however, saw a turning point in Irish history, with the development of resistance to Home Rule in Ulster to a stage of irrevocable commitment to unconstitutional force in the final analysis. It was also the year of Connolly's hasty departure from Belfast, as he received a summons that August from Dublin to take a leading role against the mass lockout of ITWU members by the federated employers of that city. (See chapter 2 below.) However, the 'Ulster crisis', as it developed from the time of the Home Rule Bill's appearance on the Commons Order Paper in April 1912 until the outbreak of world war in August 1914, radically altered the political situation in Ireland and hence Connolly's perspective on the tactics to be followed by the revolutionary socialist movement in the country. In particular, this meant a shift in emphasis from democratic forms of struggle towards the *methods*, as well as the inspiration, of the insurgent tradition in Irish revolutionary history.

With the passing of the Home Rule Bill (or, more properly,

the Government of Ireland Bill) by the Commons in the summer of 1912, it had gone to the Lords, who had promptly applied the two-sessional suspensory veto to which their powers had been reduced by the 1911 Parliament Act. Thenceforward, the bill became the target of vehement opposition from Irish Unionists, North and South, whose chief spokesman was Sir Edward Carson, MP for Dublin University and chairman of the Ulster Unionist Council. Allied to the unionist forces was the Conservative opposition, headed by Andrew Bonar Law. For Bonar Law's party, the Home Rule proposal appeared as a malevolent attempt to dismantle the empire by a Liberal administration which had already committed near treason by its disturbance of the constitutional balance through the operation of the Parliament Act. In this situation, extra-constitutional means of resistance were readily considered by the Conservative-Unionist alliance. At this early stage there was as yet no serious thought given to a partition or exclusion compromise for Ulster Protestants: Ulster was rather regarded as the rock upon which the government's whole Irish policy – and with luck its entire credibility – would founder.

In September 1912 the Ulster Covenant was signed by thousands of Protestant Ulstermen, who pledged themselves to resist the Home Rule 'conspiracy' by '. . . all means which may be found necessary'. Meanwhile, plans were already afoot for the formation of a 'provisional government' by the Unionist Council and an irregular volunteer force, designed to enforce its authority, began recruiting among Covenant signatories. By the summer of 1913, this Ulster Volunteer Force numbered 100,000 men and had been placed under the unified command of an experienced retired officer, Lt.-General Sir George Richardson. The Ulster example prompted similar measures on the part of Irish nationalists impatient with the apparent haplessness of the government in face of these unconstitutional developments in the North. In October 1913, an Irish Volunteer movement was initiated in Dublin by active cultural nationalists, chief among them being Professor Eoin MacNeill, an eminent Celtic scholar and leading figure in the Gaelic language movement. The next month the ITWU's own self-defence force, the Citizen Army, paraded for the first time. Organised initially as a means of protecting union pickets and meetings from the increasingly violent excesses of the police as the lock-out dragged on, this force also had a potential political role to play in relation to the Ulster Volunteer Force. From the outset, Connolly openly stated it might be held in readiness for use against Carson's irregulars should their extra-constitutional manoeuvrings continue unchecked in the future.[38]

This hint of a readiness to resort to armed force – albeit only as a final recourse and under extreme extra-constitutional provocation – was a telling indication of the degree to which reactionary events in these crowded years would force a crucial adjustment of Connolly's approach. It had been Connolly's doctrine that the modern phase of the Irish revolutionary struggle – that of the agricultural labourer and industrial worker for socialism – would not involve armed force or insurgency: the revolutionary ballot, supported by the economic power of the revolutionary industrial union would be the sole and sufficient weapon of the Irish workers under the Home Rule constitution. Modern socialism, Connolly pointed out, had abandoned the method of 'unfortunate insurrectionism'[39], but as he was fully aware, conditions in contemporary Ireland were in many respects far from 'modern', as the bizarre evolution of the Ulster crisis testified. In Belfast, in the summer of 1913, he reported that the task of socialist agitation amounted to ' . . . the propagation of twentieth century revolutionism amidst the mental atmosphere of the early seventeenth century'.[40] It was this contradiction, taken together with the actual recruitment of an irregular army in Ulster ready to back a 'provisional government' dedicated to the political ideals of the Reformation, which obliged Connolly to consider the supposedly outmoded form of armed struggle.

In 1913, prior to the first word of the partition proposal and prior to the outbreak of imperialist world war, Ireland's peculiar constitutional crisis had already begun to threaten the stability of the bourgeois state form. As Liberal rulers trusted to subtlety in government to preserve stability and refused to move against the para-militarists, the loyalty of their own regular forces in Ireland was already being undermined by Unionist sympathisers. As events evolved toward a politico-military confrontation between the forces of Reformation and of secular nationalism, Connolly had to prepare for any eventuality – socialist labour's attitude in the case of civil war included. As he faced the mounting pressure of the Unionist agitation and intimidation in Belfast and attempted to maintain his 'Hibernicising' drive in the post-Walker Northern socialist movement, he remained resolute in his conviction that

> . . . A real socialist movement can only be born of struggle, of uncompromising affirmation of the faith that is in us. Such a movement infallibly gathers to it every element of rebellion and progress, and in the midst of the storm and stress of the struggle solidifies into a real revolutionary force.[41]

In the storm and stress of the crisis to break upon him in the next two years, it would become increasingly clear that the nature of the real revolutionary force would have to be one capable of waging armed struggle.

2. Syndicalism: Marxism-De Leonism and Beyond

Connolly's drive toward 'Hibernicising' marxism, aiming to root the claims of historical science in the Irish revolutionary nationalist tradition, was a commitment he pursued from his earliest days as a leader of an independent socialist party in Dublin. And, as we have seen, he argued this approach initially as the basis of the reformist/parliamentarian and educational programme of the ISRP. This Irish party was conceived in the typical Second International mould: a propagandist group designed to preach the marxist message with a reformist electoral programme designed to concentrate mass political force for legislative change. However, towards the turn of the century, the actual nature and effectiveness of the conventional socialist party became problematic in itself. To some socialists, it seemed that electing socialist members to state legislatures merely served to constrain revolutionary forces within the legal framework of the democratic structure, without touching the freedom enjoyed by bourgeois governments or capitalist private enterprises. In the English-speaking world, the well-established trade union movement was an added political irritant in many respects. As an organisation of skilled workers, it was socially conservative, or at best mildly reformist, and unreservedly hostile to the marxist revolutionary programme. It was also in its own way a highly respectable political prop for the bourgeois regime. Given the impasse of parliamentary method and the highly problematic nature of relations between the marxists and the upper stratum of the proletariat, the problem of socialist organisation and strategy assumed greater urgency for some of the more reflective social democrats, Connolly included. To them it seemed that a revolutionary theory demanded a more distinct revolutionary stand both in politics and in the actual domain of the class struggle between capital and labour – the workplace and the production process. With the American theorist Daniel De Leon showing the way, these concerns evolved a distinct syndicalist organisational method. The elaboration and refinement of this methodology would become a prime commitment for Connolly, pursued jointly with his theoretical work to accomodate marxism to the Irish nationalist tradition, in the years leading up to the outbreak of the first world war.

The theoretically-based forms of syndicalism/industrial unionism which appeared within the socialist movements of the English-speaking world around the turn of the century embodied a theory of revolutionary practice unique in the marxist tradition. The syndicalist 'One Big Union' (OBU) movement, in which Connolly worked while in the USA, sought to mobilise all grades of workers in a single revolutionary union organisation. This OBU structure was conceived as the vehicle of revolutionary practice and the agency of working-class industrial and political hegemony in that post-revolutionary 'Co-operative Commonwealth' which would succeed the bourgeois state. Connolly's adherence to this American 'Marxist-De Leonist' line should be seen as the mature commitment of a social democrat for whom the Second International formula of marxist propaganda *cum* gradualist parliamentary politics had become an outmoded (indeed reactionary) approach. National OBUs, based upon the American parent body, the Industrial Workers of the World, appeared throughout the English-speaking world during the first decade of the twentieth century in Australasia, Canada, Great Britain and Ireland. The OBU movement was not a unified or homogeneous one and included both marxist and non-marxist elements, together with pro- and anti-parliamentary wings. Marxist 'politicals' like Connolly regarded parliamentary action as a necessary complement to the OBU's weapon of the revolutionary mass strike: while the OBU would thus 'take and hold' the industrial infra-structure, a democratic coup by the working-class vote would seize legitimate command of the legislature and neutralise the coercive power of the state.

In part, the emergence of the OBU movement was one response to the concrete failures of social-democratic reformism and of conventional 'craft' trade unionism to offer any real defence (let alone improvement) of working-class conditions during the 'great depression' of the final decades of the nineteenth century. From the theoretical point of view, the prime factor was the appearance in 1894 of the third volume of *Capital*, in which Marx argued that post-capitalist production would be directed by 'the associated labourers' themselves. According to Marx, the management function in the production process,

> . . . originates from the social form of the labour process, from combination and co-operation of many in pursuance of a common result; it is just as independent as that form itself as soon as it has burst its capitalistic shell.[1]

Marx hints that after the production process has outgrown the shell of capitalist relations, labour will be self-governing and co-operatively organised: co-operative factories will overcome the contradiction between capital and labour by:

> . . . making the associated labourers into their own capitalist; i.e. by enabling them to use the means of production for the employment of their own labour. They show how a new mode of production naturally grows out of an old one, when the development of the material forces of production and of the corresponding forms of social production have reached a particular stage.[2]

Marx's vision of post-capitalist relations of production is one of the 'associated labourers' becoming the embodiment of working capital. Capital and labour will be reduced to technical elements in the common productive process and will not be identified with *social* forms (i.e. capitalist and labouring classes). The investment and management functions previously carried on by the specialist capitalist class would now be conducted by the workers themselves, through such organisations as they had perfected at their workplaces and in their industries. It is in this sense that the third volume of *Capital* may be regarded as the marxist authority for the syndicalist/industrial unionist scheme of action.

The most developed form of working-class organisation then in being was that of the trade union movement. Both in North America and in the British Isles, trade unionism antedated and developed quite independently of, the marxist socialist movement. It was axiomatic within mainstream British social democracy – and accepted by Connolly himself when he worked for the British movement in Edinburgh – that trade unions were incorrigible bulwarks of capitalism and of absolutely no value, as an organisational mode, for socialist mobilisation.[3] It was during his early years in Dublin, while organising his Irish Socialist Republican Party, that Connolly's response to the third volume of *Capital* led him to re-examine these assumptions about trade unionism. When, in August 1898, Dublin trade unionists decided to sponsor 'labour' candidates in the first elections to the Irish local authorities to be instituted in the new year, Connolly welcomed this new development in working-class consciousness. He anticipated that, once workers' representatives were active on such government bodies:

> the next step in the intellectual development of the worker will be to consider . . . whether there is indeed any useful function performed by the capitalist and landlord class which the organised workers cannot perform without them [and] whether the ownership of property cannot be vested in the organised community, *and the conduct of industry entrusted to our trade unions . . .*[4]

Clearly, Connolly's notion of the supervision of the production process by labour unions is predicated on Marx's description of post-capitalist conditions in *Capital* Volume 3. However, this early move toward a syndicalist commitment from 1898, although a radical break with social democratic orthodoxy, showed only that Connolly now admitted the importance of industrial organisation for revolutionary purposes. It was the theoretical work of Daniel De Leon – leader of the marxist Socialist Labor Party of America – which would show him how the potential of trade unionism might give rise to a new kind of revolutionary practice.

The fraternal links between the struggling ISRP and the American SLP were steadily strengthening at this time. Not only was there a regular exchange of propaganda material (notable in this connection were Connolly's written appeals to Irish-American voters for use in SLP electoral campaigns), but the larger and richer American party did on occasion provide the diminutive ISRP with valuable financial aid.[5] Intellectually, Connolly's exposure at this time to De Leon's critique of the craft form of labour unionism and to his concept of party structure and discipline, proved to be a turning point in his career as a socialist activist. De Leon was then developing a critique of craft unionism in terms of the *political* potential inherent in class-conscious industrial unionism. Notably in his booklet *What Means This Strike?*, published in February 1898, De Leon condemned what he called 'pure and simple' [craft] trade unionism, pointing out its inability either to improve the workers' lot or to prevent depression of wages. Moreover, their craft structure divided workers of one skill from another and, more generally, all skilled workers from the unskilled. Hence these unions both vitiated working-class solidarity and hampered the growth of a genuine all-embracing proletarian class consciousness. Officered by 'labor fakirs' who organised support for reformist capitalist parties at the polls, these unions were weak because of their political inertia and dependence. In De Leon's view, the only form of unionisation of any value would be organisations with a class-conscious commitment to the political end of socialism. His scheme of action centred on a policy of 'dual unionism': the establishment of socialist *industrial* unions as rivals to the older craft bodies, and subordinate to the party machine. To this end, the 'Socialist Trade and Labor Alliance' (ST & LA) had been instituted as a client union of the American SLP. The revolutionary value of the industrial as opposed to the craft form of unionisation De Leon held to be self-evident: industrial unions afforded a more effective mechanism of mobilisation and control, supposedly matching the contemporary concentrations of corporate capitalism itself; craft unions he regarded as obsolescent features from the period of expansionist entrepreneurial capitalism which embodied sectional and competitive interests inimical to the collective proletarian ethic.

In thus grasping the nettle of the problem of the relations between class-conscious socialists and the established trade union movement, De Leon had approached an issue vital for American and British social democracy. In both contexts, the mutual distrust between socialists and trade unionists vitiated the impact of marxist propaganda and had led to an actual division of the socialist movement. De Leon's party, with its principled opposition to the 'fakirism' of the established union structure and its dual union alternative, was itself opposed by a reformist American Social Democratic Party which actively sought trade union support for its own electoral campaigns. This latter was analogous to the policy stand of the British Independent Labour Party: the British marxists of the Social Democratic Federation reserved their position, but ambiguously avowed themselves ready to co-operate with trade union electoral candidacies where these were run 'on socialist lines'. These standpoints had important political implications. Reformist socialists both in Britain and in the US tended to identify political revolution with evolutionary practice in a positivist, 'Darwinian' way. Hence their readiness to establish organic connections with the established 'bourgeois' parties. American reformists and union leaders looked to the Democratic Party; while the British ILP and TUC (with the marxists of the SDF in train) cultivated the Liberals in the interests of 'Labour Representation'. Now it could be argued that such politicking merely served to channel the workers' movement toward a formalistic subservience to the institutions of the bourgeois state, and it was in this regard that De Leon advanced his own concept of party.

De Leon demanded that the party be the 'incarnation of principle' and as 'intolerant as science'. In his view, it was only under the guidance of a doctrinally pure and disciplined party that the working class might be saved from the 'miseducation' of untheoretical radical reformers and from the 'opportunist' leadership of the craft unions with their bourgeois political affiliations.[6] The principled sectarianism of these demands for organisational and doctrinal exclusivity signalled a critical disagreement between De Leon and orthodox social democracy on the issue of the marxist theory of the state. From the time of Ferdinand Lassalle's leadership of the German workers' franchise struggles of the 1860s, European social democracy had come to adopt the formula of the democratic state as *patron* of working-class emancipation. It was precisely against this view that Marx wrote his *Critique of the Gotha Programme* of 1875, asserting the character of the state as a dependent function of social class, by analogy with the Roman concept of 'dictatorship'. Marx complained of the Lassallean view that:

> . . . instead of treating existing society . . . as the basis of the existing state . . . it treats the state rather as an independent entity that possesses its own intellectual, ethical and libertarian bases.[7]

Marx hastened to point out that the democratic values of the working-class movement should on no account be confused with the form of the democratic republic. This was simply '. . . the last form of state of bourgeois society'[8] within which the final class struggle of capital and labour would be fought. Thereafter, the 'state' would simply be the political will of the victorious working class: as in the ancient Roman Republic, in time of crisis, extraordinary powers of dictatorship were given to one man, setting aside all constitutional and legal forms; so, in the transitional period of crisis between capitalist and communist society, a proletarian dictatorship would transcend all bourgeois constitutional forms.[9] De Leon's sectarianism was the ultimate rejection of the Lassallean patron state theory; the assertion of the *principle* of the working class against all bourgeois social and political forms. To this end, he attacked that intrusion of bourgeois values into the workers' movement that he identified in craft unionism and he sought to expose the absolute credibility afforded the bourgeois state form by the operations of reformist social democrats and labour leaders. Above all, he opposed the demand for 'palliatives' – statutory improvements in the conditions and remuneration of labour – and had these demands deleted from the SLP programme. Orthodox social democrats believed such measures – granted and enforced by the state on petition of the workers' representatives – to be genuinely 'progressive' moves toward socialism. For De Leon, they were a kind of political heresy.

By the end of the 1890s, Connolly's own position had hardened into a De Leonite sectarianism. He publicly condemned the ideological shortcomings of the political nominees of the Irish craft unions. His severe judgment upon the municipal representatives of the Dublin trade unions was that they were:

> . . . chosen on the same lines as the middle class members, nominated by the same committee and running on the same programme. All of them hold the same political and social beliefs as the remainder of the Municipal Council – believe equally with them in the capitalist system and that rent, profit and interest are the necessary and inevitable pillars of society.[10]

The most striking example of Connolly's absorption of De Leonite views is to be found in his revision – for republication by the American SLP – of his first sustained written work, *Erin's Hope*. In the first (1897) version of the booklet published in Dublin by the ISRP, the sanguine emphasis upon parliamentary reformism and upon gradualist pressure for legislated 'palliatives' indicated how close Connolly remained to his Scottish social democratic background. He then urged upon the Irish *people* [sic] the strategy of 'open public organisation' with a view to constitutional agitation for reforms such as nationalisation of credit and transport facilities; state investment in agricultural services; statutory control of the hours of labour; state subsidies for feeding necessitous children; all of which could be achieved '. . . while there is a rag of the constitution left'.[11] In the 1902 SLP version, the palliatives together with the constitutional optimism had given place to a more abstract assertion of the sectarian principle.

> The Irish working class must emancipate itself and, in emancipating itself, it must perforce, free its country . . . This necessitates a political system of the most absolute democracy and in establishing that necessary political system, the working class must grapple with and destroy every vestige of every form of government which could interfere with the most unfettered control by the people of Ireland of all the resources of their country . . . the first actions of a revolutionary army must harmonise in principle with those likely to be its last and, therefore . . . no revolutionists can safely invite the co-operation of men or classes whose ideals are not theirs and whom therefore, they may be compelled to fight at some future critical stage

> . . . the freedom of the working class must be the work of the working class.[12]

Connolly's gradual evolution toward De Leon's sectarian position should therefore be seen as a development from the Lassallean-democratic notion of the state, to a class line which recognised in state power an instrument of proletarian self-emancipation and not an independent principle. Perhaps the best illustration of the point may be found in the eruption of the Millerand scandal within the international socialist movement at the Paris congress of the International in 1900. In 1898, Millerand, a socialist Deputy in the French National Assembly, accepted a cabinet post in the Waldeck-Rousseau government, an administration which also included General Gallifet, notorious 'butcher' of the insurgent Communards of 1871. Millerand was motivated partly by a hope of being better placed to help the unfortunate Dreyfus, but even more, perhaps, by the longstanding French Radical parliamentarian value of the overriding need in time of political stress to 'defend the republic' at all costs. In the so-called 'Kautsky resolution', the International congress gave its qualified approval for this socialist defence of radical-liberal values, and this decision subsequently came to be regarded by the socialist ultra-left as a charter for reformist policy and 'opportunist' tactics. Connolly's ISRP delegation had associated itself firmly with that of the SLP in roundly denouncing Millerand's action. The British SDF took the contrary view that such an action embodied permissible socialist tactics, and that no issue of principle was involved. The principle involved, in Connolly's view, was simply the marxist – as opposed to the Lassallean – theory of the state. He urged the SDF to recognise what was at stake and to adhere to the class line urged against the Kautsky resolution at Paris, namely: ' . . . that the revolutionary proletariat should, through its delegates, accept no governmental position which it cannot conquer by its own strength at the ballot box'.[13]

To Connolly, orthodox social democracy seemed crippled by its inability to distinguish between the *form* of the Liberal parliamentary framework and the *substance* of that 'absolute democracy' he had himself argued as an essential for working-class mobilisation in *Erin's Hope*. He became convinced that only the De Leonist approach to class-conscious action held the solution to such lack of clarity. After the Paris congress he sought to radicalise the British social democratic movement in these terms, both through direct criticism of the official leadership in his own journal, the *Workers' Republic* and by allowing De Leonite sympathisers within the British movement use of his own ISRP press. De Leonite sympathisers were particularly numerous in the SDF's Scottish branches and it was for these comrades that Connolly printed a monthly paper, the Edinburgh *Socialist*, which first appeared in August 1902. It was in this British De Leonite organ that Connolly argued his case on the Lassallean and constitutional issue in more explicit terms. On the occasion of the state visit to Britain of President Loubet of France during the summer of 1903, both the ILP and SDF leadership had welcomed the event as a portent of peace and as a testament to the growth of 'progressive' democratic sentiment among the British people. Connolly urged social democrats to guard against a facile enthusiasm for republican democracy *per se*, without regard for the actual property relations upon which that political form might subsist. The French Republic he instanced as, '. . . a bulwark of economic conservatism, and an ally of the most brutal reaction . . . the revolutionary tradition has departed from France, and, . . . her rulers have finally merged themselves in the ruck of European exploiters'.[14]

The Millerand case again provided Connolly with an opportunity to expose the theoretical unclarity of the British social democratic leaders. While refusing to condemn *in principle* Millerand's acceptance of a cabinet post, the SDF leadership denounced his *continued presence* in the French government beyond the duration of the political crisis which he gave as his original justification. Contrasting this view with the SDF's response to Loubet's visit, Connolly thundered, 'Why all this denunciation of the servant and such effusive praise of the master?'[15]

Connolly had become the leading exponent of the 'Marxist-De Leonist' line in the British Isles, but his hopes of a mass conversion of British social democracy from within were disappointed. Early in 1903, his own ISRP collapsed in factious in-fighting between reformists and De Leonites, while in April,

Scottish De Leonites were purged in a body from the SDF and constituted themselves as the nucleus of a British SLP with its headquarters in Edinburgh. This tiny party, of which Connolly became national organiser, immediately committed itself in principle to the formation of a socialist 'dual union' industrial arm on the lines of the American Socialist Trade and Labor Alliance. Connolly devoted his energies to propagandist and organisational work for the new British party throughout that summer, but its paucity of resources prevented its being able to guarantee his salary on any long-term basis. When his financial situation became desperate, Connolly determined on emigration. In September he took passage for the USA and settled in New York State, the heartland of the American SLP's strength.[16]

The basic principle of the De Leonite approach was the absolute primacy given to correctness and clarity of theory above all other matters of a merely practical, tactical or immediate nature. Connolly's adherence to this standpoint had resulted from his personal, highly strict reading of authoritative marxist texts. Once in the USA, this same insistence upon the letter of textual verity would lead him into a prolonged dispute with De Leon himself. This dispute involved critical disagreement on the questions of marriage, religion and wages: it is the wages issue however, which most concerns the present argument. The point of contention was the question of whether wage increases were necessarily nullified by a resultant automatic rise in prices: this formulation – so reminiscent of the so-called 'iron law' of minimum wages (again a theory associated with Lassalle) – was an accepted canon of the American SLP's ideology. Connolly observed: ' . . . the theory that a rise in prices always destroys the value of a rise in wages sounds very revolutionary, but it is not true . . . it is no part of our doctrine'.[17]

He appealed to the authority of Marx's *Value, Price and Profit* to exorcise this heresy, and De Leon replied insisting that wages would always level out to the value of labour power, no matter what 'ups and downs' there might be in adjustment of remuneration: this however, ignored a vital elaboration on the basic point at issue by Marx himself.[18] Marx had maintained that, in addition to the physical element – 'the necessaries absolutely indispensable for living and multiplying'[19] – there was an historical and social element. Hence:

> . . . you will find that the *value of labour* itself is not a fixed, but a variable magnitude, even supposing the values of all other commodities to remain constant. For this reason . . . although we can fix the minimum of wages, we cannot fix their *maximum*.[20]

Clearly, in terms of what Marx had actually argued, Connolly's standpoint was the correct one; nor did the concrete organisational implications of De Leon's approach escape him. He pointed out that such a wage doctrine, ' . . . knocks the feet from under the ST & LA and renders that body little else than a mere ward-heeling club for the SLP'.[21]

De Leon's approach to the wage issue cannot be divorced from consideration of the marked decline of trade in the industrialised world in the final decades of the nineteenth century. This 'Great Depression' seemed to presage a dramatic fulfilment of that immiseration process suggested by Marx himself in *Wage Labour and Capital*. In De Leon's view, the workers could not arrest this decline through combination against their employers: the best that might be expected from labour unions was action as a braking mechanism on the *rate* of decline toward what he described as an ultimate 'coolie stage' of wage labour.[22] In *Reform or Revolution* and *What Means This Strike?*, De Leon had advanced his interpretation of the failure of the 'pure and simple' trade unions to cope with the prolonged depression and, in the face of this demonstrable failure of the methods of economic struggle, had demanded *political* action by unionised labour-organisation in support of the SLP. Hence the utility of the De Leonite industrial arm, the ST & LA did not lie in its potential for economic struggle at all, but in its political function as an industrial support for the party. This union remained as the 'shaft' to which the party spear 'head' was fixed: it was essentially a political auxiliary.

The lance analogy was drawn out in a further polemical work by De Leon on the issue, *The Burning Question of Trades Unionism*, first published in 1904. With the appearance of this booklet, the De Leonite rationale of dual unionism was completed; and De Leonism so constituted properly implied as strong a rejection of the revolutionary value of economic struggle alone as anything to be found in Lenin's *What Is To Be Done?* It was in the context of De Leon's own struggle against the forms and ideology of 'economism' that the Lassallean wage doctrine was revived, as a necessary theoretical function of the subordination of the socialist union to party control. De Leon's schema for a peaceful road to socialism centred upon the party's geographical-territorial principle of organisation, itself a necessary reflection of bourgeois politics. Revolutionary mobilisation had to assume this pattern in order to assault the legislative and executive organs of the state – the seat of the coercive power of the ruling capitalist class – and this task should be undertaken by the party independently of industrial concerns or organisation.[23] This explicit reduction of the value of industrial struggle and organisation to a mere dependent role did not exclude the notion that post-revolutionary government would be 'industrialist' in complexion, when 'industrial constituencies' were expected to replace political ones: nor did it underrate the importance of the industrial union's power should the bourgeoisie refuse to recognise the victory of the socialist party at the polls. In that eventuality, the union would apply the quietus measure of the general strike, the 'general lock-out of the capitalist class' to enforce the revolutionary decision of the popular vote.[24] These considerations notwithstanding, the client relationship between party and union, together with the exclusive concern for the union's *political* role, led to that extreme pacifism in the conduct of industrial disputes which became a hallmark of De Leonite industrial unions.[25]

Dual unionism so conceived signified the ultimate divorce of the revolutionary principle from the actual labour movement; indeed it posed a direct, structural antagonism between them. On the simplest view, this position clearly runs into difficulties regarding Marx's formulations in the *Manifesto* relative to the relations between proletarians and communists:

> The Communists do not form a separate party, opposed to other working class parties.

> They have no interests separate and apart from those of the Proletariat as a whole.
>
> They do not set up any sectarian principles of their own, by which to shape and mould the proletarian movement.[26]

The De Leonite sect had theory alone: it was class consciousness without the organised working class. This was more than a merely formal contradiction: De Leon's theory of the state consisted in the principle of class consciousness articulated as a political idea, but his dual unionism and wage theories precluded any self-actualisation of that idea in practice. Connolly opposed De Leon's contradictory approach on wages both in 1904 and again in mid-January of 1907 when the SLP's national executive endorsed this stand as official policy: on this second occasion Connolly was hounded out of the party for his theoretical deviance from SLP orthodoxy on this, as well as on normative/ethical issues.* However, by the time he was obliged in this way to part company with the De Leonite sect, concrete developments within the labour movement itself suggested to Connolly an organisational form with real potential to *embody* class consciousness in its own political practice.

At a gathering of industrial unionists convened in Chicago in January 1905, a new departure in labour organisation was made with the formation of the 'Industrial Workers of the World'. This syndicalist labour union had been established with the avowed aim of organising all grades of workers into 'One Big Union' (OBU). In its *Manifesto* the new body spelled out its organisational scheme:

> . . . one great industrial union embracing all industries – providing for craft autonomy locally, industrial autonomy internationally, and working class unity generally . . . founded on the class struggle and . . . [upon] . . . the recognition of the irrepressible conflict between the capitalist class and the working class.[27]

This rationale is an admixture of trades unionism, anarchism and marxism; but in addition to the anarchist-*cum*-marxist

*The normative/ethical dispute is examined in chapter 4.

rhetoric, there was included an absolute condemnation of craft unionism as a 'worn-out and corrupt system'. The craft union mode was castigated for its inability to end wage-slavery, its effectiveness in perpetuating divisions within the working class, its assistance to the employers in the creation of trades monopolies and its role in fostering political ignorance and hindering the growth of class consciousness among the workers. The whole tone of the *Manifesto* is shot through with the sombre tenor of Marx's *Wage Labour and Capital*: 'there is no silver lining to the clouds of darkness and despair settling down upon the world of labor', it averred. This vision was modified – though unbrightened – by consideration of the role of employers' combinations and the domination of modern industry by automation and trusts. The *Manifesto* asserted:

> The *great facts* of present industry are the displacement of human skill by machines and the increase of capitalist power through concentration in the possession of the tools with which wealth is produced and distributed . . . Class divisions grow ever more fixed and class antagonisms more sharp. Trade lines have been swallowed up in a common servitude of all workers to the machines which they tend. New machines, ever replacing less productive ones, wipe out whole trades and plunge new bodies of workers into the ever growing army of tradeless, hopeless unemployed.[28]

For the Chicago industrial unionists, it was axiomatic that craft unionism – and indeed the entire structure of craft-differentiated industrial labour – would be numbered among the inevitable casualties of the accelerated productivity of maturing capitalism, as outlined in *Wage Labour and Capital*. Loss of trade skills would be one prime function of proletarian immiseration.

In general terms, syndicalism may be said to have its origins in the anarchism that was so deplored by the marxist socialists of both the First and Second Internationals, yet which clung – incubus like – to their organisations. Syndicalism may be regarded as the accommodation of this 'anti-political heresy' to the labour movement, best typified perhaps by those autonomous *syndicats* which combined to form the French *Confédération*

Générale de Travail (CGT) in 1902.[29] These syndicalist organisations rejected the orthodox state socialism of the social democratic movement, being hostile to political action; but accepted the marxist critique of capitalist economics and bourgeois society. The IWW may be seen as a North American counterpart of the CGT, although it would differ from the latter in the important respect of developing a much more centralised organisational structure. One of the many constituent elements of the IWW was the ST & LA, and at this early period of the new body's life, Daniel De Leon became its leading ideologue.[30] De Leon's attempt to modify his dual unionist position to accommodate the organised class consciousness embodied in the IWW is crucial for an understanding of Connolly's further ideological development. De Leon now accorded the OBU equal status to that of the party, each being mutually dependent essentials in working-class organisation for the overthrow of capitalism.[31] In the post-revolutionary 'Industrial Commonwealth', sovereignty would fall to the central administrative organs of the OBU, the political state having 'withered away' or, in De Leon's formulation, 'Where the General Executive Board of the Industrial Workers of the World will sit, there will be the nation's capital.'[32]

The OBU was charged in this new rationale with the task of ideological supervision of the party; a critical innovation and a value to which Connolly consistently adhered thereafter. As De Leon put it, '. . . nothing short of a . . . [class-conscious] . . . economic organisation can keep sharp the edge of the special sword wielded by the political movement of labor'.[33]

Given this strategy, a peaceful revolution was assured in the USA – something impossible in Europe[34] – and the OBU remained to support the party with the ultimate sanction of the 'general lock-out of the capitalist class'.[35] The tasks of the OBU as thus elaborated by De Leon must be seen in relation to the highly-structured organisation of the IWW; particularly so with regard to its supervisory and administrative role in the projected post-revolutionary 'Industrial Commonwealth'. The structure provided for thirteen international industrial divisions ('departments') supposedly matching the current achievement of the concentration of capitalist forms of production: these 'departments' were further divided into national industrial unions comprised of area locals (branches) in the normal way. A General Executive Board (G.E.B.) presided over the departments, exercising general administrative and financial control throughout the organisation, controlling the OBU's press and vested with ultimate veto power over all subordinate echelons in the structure. The G.E.B. could also call any part of tne OBU out on strike without any kind of ballot. There was provision for an element of territorial organisation in the form of District Industrial Councils, intermediate between the locals and the G.E.B. and functional in parallel to the national and departmental structures. Each echelon was controlled by its own executive; while ultimate authority rested in the annual international convention, with provision for a referendum of the general membership beyond that.[36] At its 1906 convention, the IWW incorporated into its constitution a principle directly taken from *Capital* Volume 3; namely that, 'By organising industrially, we are forming the structure of the new society, within the shell of the old.'[37]

From the time of his resignation from the SLP in 1907, Connolly concentrated his energies in organisational work for the IWW (becoming its New York district organiser) and, from 1909, in full-time work for the (reformist) Socialist Party of America. His theoretical development now proceeded from De Leon's schematic accommodation to the reality of the IWW structure as outlined above and later published in booklet form as *The Socialist Reconstruction of Society*. When in 1908, the 'bummery' coup within the IWW ejected De Leon and the ST & LA element (together with all 'politics') from the organisation, Connolly remained; a De Leonist in a 'pure' anti-political syndicalist union. His *primary* commitment to the IWW as the structural embodiment of organised class consciousness remained absolute and he now followed two courses of action: within the IWW he urged the necessity of political action – mobilising the working-class vote in support of candidates approved by the industrial union; while within the Socialist Party he argued that only the industrial union principle could adequately organise the working class for the revolutionary tasks of social democracy. These were twin themes in his first sustained programmatic work *Socialism Made Easy*, published by Charles Kerr & Co. of Chicago in 1909. This was actually a highly derivative work and in essence a restatement of De Leon's position as argued in his *The Socialist Reconstruction of Society*. Connolly merely added evidence drawn from European and Irish history and Scandinavian industrial experience as material illustrative of De Leon's arguments. The basic premise of this work was taken whole from De Leon; namely that a revolutionary political unity could alone come about as a function of working-class industrial unity, as realised through the collectivity of the OBU. Class-conscious political and economic mobilisation should proceed in parallel:

> . . . the fight for the conquest of the political state is not the battle, it is only the echo of the battle. The real battle is the battle being fought out every day for the power to control industry, and the gauge of the progress . . . [made] . . . is not to be found in the number of voters making a cross beneath the symbol of a political party, but in the number of those workers who enrol themselves in an industrial organisation with the definite purpose of making themselves masters of the industrial equipment of society in general.
>
> That battle will have its political echo: that industrial organisation will have its political expression. *If we accept the definition of working-class political action as that which brings the workers as a class into direct conflict with the possessing class* AS A CLASS, *and keeps them there, then we must realise that* NOTHING CAN DO THAT SO READILY AS ACTION AT THE BALLOT BOX. Such action . . . emphasises the class character of the Labor movement. IT IS THEREFORE ABSOLUTELY INDISPENSABLE FOR THE EFFICIENT TRAINING OF THE WORKING CLASS ALONG CORRECT LINES, THAT ACTION AT THE BALLOT BOX SHOULD ACCOMPANY ACTION IN THE WORKSHOP.[38]

However, the concept of party implied by Connolly's scheme of mobilisation was far from the De Leonite one of a theoretically 'pure' and disciplined elite. In his view, the growth of the IWW had vindicated the more 'tolerant' and gradualist orientation of the SPA. He declared:

> . . . that since the political party was not to accomplish the revolution but only to lead the attack upon the political citadel of Capitalism, there no longer existed the same danger in the unclearness of its membership, nor compelling necessity for insisting upon its purification . . . it is our belief there will evolve . . .
>
> One Socialist party, embracing all shades and conceptions of Socialist political thought.
>
> One Socialist industrial organisation drilling the working class for the supreme mission of their class – the establishment of the Workers' Republic.[39]

This 'mass line' approach to questions of revolutionary discipline and leadership, Connolly based quite explicitly upon the principle of democratic centralism: he formally distinguished it from that bureaucratic centralism he saw as inherent in the structure of the bourgeois state.

> Social Democracy . . . is the application to industry . . . of the fundamental principles of democracy. Such application will necessarily have to begin in the workshop and proceed logically . . . upward . . . until it reaches the culminating point of national executive power . . . Social Democracy must proceed from the bottom upward, whereas capitalist political society is organised from above downward . . . this conception of Socialism destroys at one blow all the fears of a bureaucratic state.[40]

Connolly summarised the new approach he was then developing to questions of organisational method in a private letter to a Scottish comrade in May 1908. He wrote:

> . . . I have come to believe that Keir Hardie was wise in his generation when he worked to form the LRC [Labour Representation Committee] and that he showed a nearer approximation to the spirit of the much-quoted phrase of Marx about the trade unions alone being able to form the political party of Labor* than any of our revolutionists (or Danites) ever did or do . . . he has demonstrated to us the

*A principle purported to come from Marx, often expounded by De Leon. He was never able to give any textual substantiation for it.

real method of upbuilding a Socialist Labor Party. What we want to do is to show that the same method can be utilised in building a revolutionary party, free from the faults and shunning the compromises of the LRC. If that body was dominated by Industrial Unionists instead of by pure and simplers; if it was elected by industrial unions and controlled entirely by them and capable *at any moment* of having its delegates recalled by the unions, and had also its mandate directly from the rank and file organised in the workshops, it would be just the party we want.[41]

For all of his attempts to come to terms with the reality of the IWW structure, De Leon had remained unclear on the issue of the OBU's tasks as a revolutionary vehicle. For Connolly the revolutionary OBU, or union 'of a new type' will perform substantially similar tasks to Lenin's party 'of a new type'. It will be the ultimate guardian of revolutionary consciousness, the vanguard organisation of the whole proletariat and the material creator of the new egalitarian order destined to succeed capitalist society. Through the workers' party – its own creature – it will exercise the political will of the working class and assume revolutionary power in the institutions of the bourgeois state, which it will then suppress. At that point in history, Connolly envisaged the operation of '. . . a State which should be a social instrument in the hands of its men and women, where state powers would be wielded as a means *by the workers* . . .'.[42] Here we find Connolly advocating something like the proletarian dictatorship first envisaged by Marx in his *Critique of the Gotha Programme* and further elaborated by Lenin in his *The State and Revolution*. From De Leon, Connolly took the notion of the proletarian revolution as a suppression of the territorial bourgeois-type of political state and its replacement with the 'industrial administration' of the OBU executive, which would then become the 'national government'.[43] Logically then, state power could not be used as a means by the workers, in Connolly's phrase, except in terms of that *interim period* between capitalist government and socialist administration. In terms both of the exercise of political power and of the conceptual timetable of revolutionary practice, Connolly's industrial union would be expected to fulfil the same 'dictatorship' role as Lenin's vanguard party. Again, like the Bolshevik party, the OBU's fitness for revolutionary mobilisation will enable it to supervise the whole process of production in the post-revolutionary state:

> With the industrial union as our principle of action, branches can be formed to give expression to the need for effective supervision of the affairs of the workshop, shipyard, dock or railway.
>
> . . . the concept of one Big Union embracing all, [is] the outline of the most effective form of combination for industrial warfare, and also for the Social Administration of the Co-operative Commonwealth of the future.[44]

However, Connolly's OBU schematic also implied a specialist separation of the political and economic arms of the workers' movement, and a voluntaristic 'mass line' notion of leadership based upon the collective militancy of the rank and file. It should be pointed out that these concepts of a divided *apparat* and of a non-hierocratic leadership are decidedly at variance with the Leninist scheme of a unified 'scientific' direction of the mass movement by trained professional cadres. Connolly did not shrink from describing his conception of socialist government in detailed form. Under socialism, the OBU structure would deal with problems of a practical sort such as economic planning, investment management, production supervision and consumer control: it would also embody the moral end and public observance of the collectivist ethic.

> Government under Socialism will be largely a matter of statistics. The chief administrative body of the nation will be a collection of representatives from the various industries and the professions. From the industries they represent these administrators will learn of the demand for the articles they manufacture: the industries will learn from the storekeepers of the national stores and warehouses what articles are demanded by the general public who purchase at these stores, and the cumulative total of the reports given by storekeepers and industries will tell the chief administrative body (Congress, if you will) how much to produce

> and where to place it to meet the demand. Likewise, the reports brought to the representatives from their Industrial Union as to the relative equipment and power of their factories in each district will enable them to place their orders in the places most suited to fill them, and to supervise and push forward the building and developing of new factories and machinery . . . When the workers elect their foremen and superintendents, and retain them only during effective supervision and handling of their allotted duties; when industries elect their representatives in the National Congress and the Congress obeys the demand emanating from the public for whom it exists, corruption and favouritism will be organically impossible.[45]

For Connolly the OBU scheme of joint political and industrial mobilisation would ensure a peaceful revolution and a *legitimate* assumption of power by the representatives of the industrial workers. The element of physical force in the historical bourgeois revolution had been significant because the needs of that class struggle could in no way be served by existent feudal institutions: the revolutionary organisation of the proletariat however, in industrial unions, was itself a function of the perfection of bourgeois economic institutions in the form of trusts. Referring to the events of the French Revolution in this light, Connolly had remarked:

> The capitalist French revolutionist had to fight to destroy the institutions of his enemy; the socialist revolutionist has to fight in order to give the economic institutions of his enemy room to grow . . .[46]

And hence:

> In the vote, the strike, the [economic] boycott and the *lock-out exercised against the master class*, the Socialists have weapons that will make this social revolution comparatively bloodless and peaceable . . .[47]

In the same way that capitalist economic structures nourished the industrial organisation of the working class, so did the legal form of the bourgeois state facilitate the open and constitutional activity of a workers' party which aimed at a legitimate seizure of political power. In order to forestall or frustrate such a democratic constitutional *coup* as that in preparation by the Socialist Party, the bourgeois leadership would itself have to resort to illegitimate means of retaining power and reduce itself to a usurping administration based upon naked coercion. Even during such a crisis, Connolly argued, the OBU structure would prevent civil war between revolutionary and counter-revolutionary forces occurring. Besides, against all the sophisticated weaponry of modern military technology, armed action on the part of the workers would be as ineffectually disastrous as it was unnecessary. There had been considerable heart-searching debate in the American Socialist Party on this question of the revolutionary ballot being 'stricken from the hands' of the party in such an unconstitutional way. It was even feared that the US Supreme Court might be used to declare the party illegal, in view of its aim being that of the overthrow of the US Constitution. Connolly asserted confidently that:

> . . . in case of a Supreme Court decision rendering illegal the political activities of the socialist party, or instructing the capitalist officials to refuse to vacate their offices after a national victory by that party, the industrially organised workers would give the usurping government a Roland for its Oliver by refusing to recognise its officers, to transport or feed its troops, to transmit its messages, to print its notices, or to chronicle its doings by working in any newspaper which upheld it. Finally, after having thus demonstrated the helplessness of capitalist officialdom in the face of united action by the producers (by attacking said officialdom with economic paralysis . . .) the industrially organised working class could proceed to take possession of the industries of the country after informing the military and other coercive forces of capitalism that they could procure the necessaries of life by surrendering themselves to the lawfully elected government and renouncing the usurpers at Washington.[48]

It should be stressed that Connolly's conception of such a legitimate road to socialism in no way implied adherence either to the form of legitimacy embodied in bourgeois politics or to legitimacy as an independent principle. For Connolly, the law, no less than the state itself, was essentially a vehicle of class rule. He was clear that successive historical class competitions for the legal and political power to exploit labour had resulted in a situation in which the last subject class – the proletariat – now found one of its most useful revolutionary weapons in its possession of the legitimate franchise.

> . . . every class in [historical] Society, from the King to the capitalist, has successively captured political power and when enthroned in possession has legalised its own conception of society. Each class has had a different method of exploiting Labour, and the fight for governmental power has been a contest in which each rising class above the working class has sought to make its own peculiar manner of appropriating the products of the labour of the workers the only lawful manner. In this fight the mechanism of government has been gradually improved and extended, and its franchises broadened down until the means of acquiring power have at last come within reach of the only remaining subject class – the workers.[49]

Connolly's position as a national organiser for the SPA he described as 'the best job I ever had in my life'; yet his thoughts were increasingly turning toward the possibility of returning to Ireland, if he could only get a living at tradesman's wages there.[50] Meanwhile he urged the SPA to establish a working relationship with the IWW and to adopt the industrial unionist solution both to the problem of working-class disunity and to that of correct political action:

> That problem [of working-class disunity] is intimately allied with the future of the Socialist Party in America. Our party must become the political expression of the fight in the workshop and draw its inspiration therefrom . . . *the most dispersive and isolating force at work in the labor movement today is craft unionism, the most cohesive and unifying force, industrial unionism*. In view of that fact, all objections which my comrades make to industrial union-

> ism on the grounds of the supposedly, or truly anti-political, bias of many members of the IWW is quite beside the mark. That question at the present stage of the game is purely doctrinaire. The use or non-use of political action will not be settled by the doctrinaires who make it their hobby today, but will be settled by the workers who use the IWW in their workshop struggles.[51]

This appeal for a non-doctrinaire approach to the vital issues of working-class mobilisation was published in February 1910, only five months prior to his final return to Ireland. Connolly had salvaged the 'industrialist' schematic from the constraints of De Leonite dogma and sectarian practice. He recognised only the legitimacy of the organised class consciousness embodied in the industrial union structure. In the succeeding years of intensifying political and industrial struggle in Ireland, he would develop this class line into a flexible and powerful organisational method.

When Connolly returned to work again in the Irish movement, the end of his syndicalist method necessarily became identified with national as well as class freedom: his post-De Leonite ideology assumed an anti-imperialist logic. He became the leading figure in the diminutive but expanding Socialist Party of Ireland: the party's programme soon came to reflect this union of the nationalist and syndicalist goals and called upon the Irish working class to ' . . . organise itself industrially and politically with the end in view of gaining control and mastery of the entire resources of the country'.[52] Connolly himself described the SPI's nature at this time as,

> . . . a party that rests upon Irish conditions, continues the traditional work for national freedom for Ireland as part of its mission and draws its inspiration from the revolutionary history of the past as well as the social development of the present.[53]

Of crucial significance was Connolly's appointment, in June 1911, as Belfast secretary of the self-styled 'Ireland's OBU', the Irish Transport Workers' Union. This was a militant mass union seeking to enrol all grades of workers employed in the transport industries. It was one element of the so-called 'Greater Unionism' latterly developing in the British Isles which sought to consolidate the unskilled and craft unions into structures of national and full industrial scope. Foremost among these unions was the Transport Federation headed by Robert Williams and Tom Mann. Mann had recently returned from Australia where he had absorbed some of the theory of the American IWW – including Connolly's work *Socialism Made Easy*. Calling himself an 'industrial syndicalist', Mann urged the case for restructuring craft and sectional unionism along federative lines with the aim of achieving a greater class solidarity among the myriad separate unions then in existence. He rejected De Leonite notions of dual unionism and regarded working through the established 'old line' union structure as the only sound approach: his chief weapon to give effect to the new solidarity was that of the sudden, sympathetic strike.[54] Jim Larkin, leader of the ITWU, was a staunch supporter of 'syndicalism' as thus understood and of the tactic of the sympathetic strike: during the course of the mass strike in 1911 by the Transport Federation, sympathetic action in Dublin by Larkin's organisation contributed much to its eventual success. However, Mann's Federation, working through autonomous 'old line' unions and ever dependent upon the good offices and co-operation of their officials, suffered from the structural weaknesses of all confederacies: the ITWU was a unitary body able to act independently within its own national orbit.

As an official of Ireland's OBU, Connolly would find something approaching an ideal opportunity to broadcast his syndicalist doctrine among the Irish working class. Although the organisation was a new and struggling one, and its base rested more on Larkin's charisma than upon sound theory or finance, it afforded Connolly a real means of integrating his theory with the practical dimension of the industrial struggle. For him it was the ultimate vehicle of *praxis*, unifying the industrial and political struggles: a forum for defining and testing the contours of a revolutionary strategy for Ireland. Conversely, his advent gave to the union a profound sense of its purpose that Larkin, lacking Connolly's conceptual abilities, could never provide. Even as a subordinate official, it was Connolly who provided the vision of the significance of the union's day-to-day fight for improved wages and conditions, in terms of the De Leonite logic of economic combination to 'expropriate' the capitalist class in industry and in the state.

Both in terms of his own developed theory and in having such a revolutionary vehicle to hand in this embryo Irish union 'of a new type', Connolly had made a definitive break with the organisational method followed in his earlier period in Ireland. While working through the old ISRP, he had conceived of the socialist agitation in terms of educational-propagandist activity, by a party of teaching adherents, lecturing and fighting elections whenever and wherever they could and backed by a tightly controlled party press. Such was the typical method of the Second International parties and, in his early years in the Irish movement, Connolly addressed himself in this fashion to a working class of disorganised unskilled men and to superior craftsmen mainly organised in branches of the British 'amalgamated' trade unions. While the unskilled then lacked the industrial organisation for real class solidarity, the superior tradesmen of the great 'amalgamateds' remained reformist and conservative in outlook and attached themselves politically to the Irish Parliamentary Party in the South, and to the Liberal Unionist cause in the North.

The eruption of the fiery Larkin onto the Irish labour scene in 1907 had brought about widespread change by the time of Connolly's return to the country. During the course of 1909, Larkin had enrolled thousands of general workers – concentrating on the dockers and carters – in the new ITWU and had begun a vigorous campaign for improved wages and conditions which increasingly put Dublin employers on the defensive. Nor was the union's influence confined to its own membership. By an extensive use of sympathetic action and through observance of 'tainted' goods, Larkin gained widespread respect and support throughout the labour movement, including the artisans of the skilled trades. The union's weekly journal edited by him, *The Irish Worker*, had achieved a higher circulation rate by 1911 than many of its nationalist equivalents. To Connolly fell the relatively thankless task of building up the union's presence in sectarian Belfast and to this he applied himself with characteristic energy and imagination: during the first month of his new appointment he won union recognition and wage increases for local dockers after taking Belfast port employers by surprise with sympathetic action in connection with the general shipping dispute. It was through active involvement in wage bargaining, sympathetic action and in writing for the *Irish Worker* that Connolly secured an attentive audience for his syndicalist teaching and example.

In parallel to these developments within the Irish labour movement, there occurred clandestine developments in the nationalist movement which were to have equally far-reaching consequences. In 1907, the veteran Fenian dynamitard Thomas Clarke returned to Dublin from the USA: ostensibly he returned to spend his last years in the homeland quietly running a small tobacconist business; but he had actually returned to revive the old Irish Republican Brotherhood, a secret society dedicated to undercover mobilisation for an armed overthrow of British authority in Ireland. Aided by his subtle and persuasive lieutenant Sean MacDermott, Clarke had succeeded within a few years in administering the Brotherhood's oath to hundreds of activists in the cultural nationalist movement. These two men and their followers would later provide much of the fighting material for the Easter Rising.

Meanwhile, the return to power at Westminster of the Liberal Party in 1905 once more placed Irish Home Rule on the government agenda: it was not however until April 1912 that an actual Bill was brought forward. In preparation for Home Rule, Connolly had worked hard to achieve a unification of socialist forces in Ireland. His efforts were largely successful and, at Easter 1912, the SPI absorbed most of the Ulster branches of the ILP to form a new Independent Labour Party of Ireland. Also on Connolly's initiative, the Irish TUC in May decided on a policy of labour representation; the sponsoring of 'Labour' candidacies at all elections. The ILP (I)'s programme for action under the new constitution was explicitly syndicalist, defining its aim as the creation of an 'Industrial Commonwealth'.

1. *Political*: Organisation of the forces of labour in Ireland to take political action on independent lines for securing the control of all public elective bodies and for the

mastery of all the public powers of the state, in order that such bodies and such powers should be used for the attainment of the above object [i.e. the Industrial Commonwealth].

2. *Industrial*: Furtherance of the industrial organisation of the wage-earners, with a view to securing unity of action in the industrial field as a means to the conquest of industrial power, the necessary preliminary to industrial freedom.[55]

On the industrial front, Connolly's continued energy built up a flourishing branch of the ITWU in Belfast and he extended his activity into the local linen trade. He succeeded in organising large numbers of linen workers into a textile workers' affiliate of the OBU. Initially he was opposed in this effort by specialist craft unions in the industry, but after receiving support while on strike from Connolly's new organisation, these craft bodies signified their own conversion to the OBU idea by themselves entering into affiliation. Sympathetic action could thus be used to enlarge the OBU structure.[56] However, no matter how successful he was on his own terms in political and industrial work in Belfast, Connolly's achievements there in the areas of socialist unity and OBU building were in many ways insubstantial. The politico-military forces of the Ulster Covenant were in the ascendant in 1912-13 and swept away much of the potential of Connolly's work in Belfast. Socialists of all persuasions, together with members of the 'Fenian' ITWU and its affiliates, were harassed in a mounting campaign of sectarian violence. A 'Protestant Workers' Association' appeared as a rival to the ITWU and, as the collapse of an aluminium workers' strike at Larne in June 1913 indicated, such Protestant membership as the OBU had gained was unable to withstand clerical and Orange pressure to withdraw from the organisation.[57] It was from this worsening situation that Connolly was summoned to Dublin in the final week of August to lead the OBU in the most severe crisis it had yet faced.

The Dublin transport workers' lock-out of 1913 was the result of the local federated employers' attempt to break up the ITWU. The shipping companies and dock employers had already felt the union's power and had been obliged to make substantial concessions to its membership. Connolly himself described the 'revolution in wages and conditions' currently underway with reference to Larkin's new approach to union tactics:

> The governing factor in winning these battles in Dublin is the fact that practically all classes of general labour are in the union, and that the leader of that union does not act . . . on old trade union lines. The general policy is to use the general body of workers who are organised in order to win concessions for those who are being organised . . . The firm and skilful use of this power is what is making for the revolution in wages and conditions in Dublin that is at present going on . . .[58]

The Dublin lock-out was the most dramatic, and certainly the most bitterly fought, of all the great labour disputes which troubled the British Isles during the period immediately prior to the first world war. As the climate of the dispute became increasingly violent both Connolly and Larkin were arrested, but were subsequently released, Connolly after spending a week on hunger strike. Police brutality during the days of August had been severe: two union members had been killed and many others, together with uninvolved citizens, had been injured during police attempts to disperse mass meetings and pickets. British appreciation of the 'syndicalism' of the ITWU tended to polarise around response to Tom Mann's concept of anti-parliamentary 'industrial syndicalism'. Connolly hastened to deny the 'superstition' of this conflation of Irish practice with that of Mann, stressing the ITWU belief that, 'The working class should be in one union, not only an industrial union, but a political union.'[59]

With this formalistic appreciation of 'syndicalism' on the simple criterion of pro- or anti-parliamentarianism in the British labour movement, there could be little understanding of Connolly's developed post-De Leonite doctrine of OBU control of both the industrial and political labour struggle. Labour politicians in Britain, notably Philip Snowden, publicly criticised the practice of the ITWU and the sympathetic strike on the grounds of its supposed political counter-productivity. Connolly replied to this criticism with the assertion that political action was a necessary and essential reflex of the industrial battle, but:

> At present . . . Labour politicians seem to be losing all reality as effective aids to our struggles on the industrial battlefields . . . [and] . . . of their true role as parliamentary outposts of the industrial army. The Parliamentary tail in Britain still persists in wagging the British industrial dog. Once the dog really begins to assert his true position, we will be troubled no more by carping critics of Labour politics . . .[60]

This contradiction between *labour politician* and *industrial militant* clearly demonstrated how orthodox social democracy continued to reflect the dualist ethic of liberal society within its own structure. Connolly was *both*: a marxist syndicalist whose practice embodied the class-conscious line of a total political-*cum*-industrial mobilisation.

By November, with Larkin again imprisoned, Connolly assumed full leadership of the union. The conflict had now escalated with his decision to establish a mass picket at all workplaces involved: the authorities responded with military protection – in addition to the police – for those firms still operating with scab labour. As armed soldiers and scabs daily confronted the mass pickets and the ITWU's own disciplined club-wielding defence force, the 'Citizen Army', the lock-out reached climax point. The Dublin strikers could do no more, and success or failure for their cause now hinged upon thorough-going sympathetic action on the part of the British trade union movement. Hostility toward (and fear of) the tactics of militant 'syndicalism' ran deep within the craft-consciousness of the British TUC leadership however, and, by December, the decision had been made to deny sympathetic industrial support. The 'fraternal' measure of chartering a food ship for the starving strikers and their families was the only tangible support offered. The collapse of the strike effort in the first weeks of 1914 followed inevitably, and this outcome profoundly strained Connolly's sense of solidarity with the British labour movement. With cold fury he denounced the 'trade union scabbery' practised upon the

Irish union and spoke of such action re-opening 'that chasm of distrust and hatred' between Irish and British workers which served so well the interests of the master class in both countries.[61] The abandonment of the ITWU by the British TUC clearly displayed the confederal weakness of the 'Greater Unionism', permeated as it was by sectional and craft-type attitudes of mind. It was in this light that Connolly sought to analyse the failure of working-class solidarity in 1913-14, urging that revolutionary fighting spirit should take priority over bureaucratic formality and warning that, in the hands of conventional trade union officials, the greater unions might become monstrous fetters upon the struggling labour movement. He urged British labour to use the strike weapon in a sporadic and surprise form, a radical tactic which, despite its unpopularity with conservative union officials, '. . . has won more for Labour than all the great Labour conflicts in history'.[62] Above all, the fate of the Dublin workers showed the necessity for,

> . . . the amalgamation of all forces of labour into one union, capable of concentrating all forces upon any one issue or in any one fight [a union which] . . . can alone fight industrially as the present development and organisation of Capital requires that Labour should fight . . .[63]

In what was to be one of his final statements on the organisational problem, Connolly mooted the idea of a centralised trade union authority – along the lines of the cabinet executive of the state – whose power might override the sectional concerns so evident within the federations of the greater unionism. This proposal – modelled on the General Executive Board of the IWW – would enhance both the organisational strength and the revolutionary consciousness of the working class.

> Out of such an arrangement the way would be opened for a more thorough organisation of the working class upon the lines of real industrial unionism . . . Whatever be our form of organisation, the spirit of sectionalism still rules and curses our class.[64]

Connolly's logic clearly implied the creation of 'One Big Union' throughout the British Isles, based upon the commercial and industrial unity achieved by corporate capitalism. Politically however, Ireland was a separate entity from Great Britain. The unique burden of its history meant that the problem of the state would have to be approached by organised labour in a distinct way appropriate to Irish conditions: national freedom was necessarily a prime goal for the Irish revolutionary union. Connolly was then searching for ways of giving creative expression to the OBU concept, both for Ireland's liberation and for the total proletarian struggle within the British Isles. However, his analytical quest was aborted in the short space of life remaining to him by the urgency of the threat of Irish partition and by the crisis of world war.

3. The Crisis: 1914-16

In the second week of March 1914 the Liberal Prime Minister, H. H. Asquith, made his 'new and final proposal' on Irish Home Rule. It amounted to a scheme of partition in Ireland, certain Ulster counties being enabled to exclude themselves from the Government of Ireland Act: this was the price with which Carson's militant unionists were to be bought off and civil war avoided. The actual proposal was that the Ulster counties be given the right to exclude themselves for a period of six years after the enactment of the new constitution and then automatically to accede to its jurisdiction unless it should be decided otherwise by the UK electorate voting in the general elections which would occur in the interim. If the Liberals went out of office during the six year period, an incoming Conservative administration could operate the scheme to its own advantage and make the exclusion permanent.

Political partition on ethno-religious lines was not an entirely new answer to the perennial 'Irish question'. Gladstone himself had discussed such a notion – without bringing forward any legislative measures to implement it – while introducing his Home Rule Bill of 1886 in the Commons. On a more practical note, the House had rejected a proposed amendment to the 1912 Bill designed to secure the exclusion of the four Ulster counties of Antrim, Down, Derry and Armagh. When Sir Edward Carson spoke to the amendment, he made it quite clear that Unionists were not interested in such a compromise, but rather insisted upon the right to an absolute *veto* over Irish Home Rule *per se*. The exclusion compromise of 1914 was the result of intensive negotiation between Asquith and Lloyd George, representing the government, and the Irish Unionist and Nationalist leaders. Having formally condemned the exclusion measure in the Commons, Carson made the crossing to Belfast on 19 March amidst fears of an immediate formation of a 'provisional government' in Ulster. The government had made some show of force with the movement of naval and military reinforcements into the province, and this was countered by the 'Curragh mutiny' of 20 March, a mass resignation of cavalry officers in Ireland sympathetic to the Ulster cause. Despite this atmosphere of impending crisis, negotiations continued between all parties concerned, and would continue all of that summer, mainly over the issues of which parts of Ulster should be given the right to exclude themselves and precisely how they should vote on the matter. The subsequent detailed bargaining apart, Carson's position in March rapidly evolved into a demand for a total exclusion of the nine counties of Ulster from the operation of the Government of Ireland Act. These areas would remain under the direct rule of the Westminster parliament, exercising a degree of 'administrative autonomy' at the local level. Formal considerations notwithstanding, Carson's position was substantially a proposal for a separate Northern polity in all practical affairs.

For Connolly, the Irish partition proposal implied a disastrous division of the native working-class movement: the forces of labour under the new constitution would be denied the support of the most 'advanced' section of the Irish proletariat in industrial Belfast; and the growing political power of labour would be checked, confirming the hegemony of the 'natural' political leaders of the Orange and Home Rule bourgeois establishments, North and South. He argued that:

> Such a scheme would destroy the Labour movement by disrupting it. It would perpetuate in a form aggravated in evil the discords now prevalent, and help the Home Rule and Orange Capitalists and clerics to keep their rallying cries before the public as the political watchwords of the day. In short, it would make division more intense and confusion of ideas and parties more confounded.[1]

Connolly had no doubt that the 'Ulster crisis' – the flight of Carson from the Commons back to Ulster, the troop movements into the province, even the subsequent 'Curragh Mutiny' – was at base a theatrical show designed to distract the working-class nationalist democracy from the full implications of the partition scheme. While leaving property relations untouched, partition boded fair to retard the political organisation and consciousness of the Irish working people and to safeguard the capitalist institutions of the British empire from the revolutionary elements of Irish nationalism. Connolly regarded acquiescence by the Irish parliamentary party in this scheme as the grossest act of betrayal it was yet guilty of against the interests of Ireland and its working people. Above all, he feared for the fate of the Catholic and nationalist community of Ulster, once it had been abandoned to the will of an Orange majority in a separate Northern state. In view of these considerations, Connolly's response to the partition proposal was from the outset a commitment in principle to armed force if necessary, to prevent its implementation.[2]

The partition issue reopened debate on Connolly's long-standing bone of contention with the political leadership of British labour; the consistent policy of the old ILP, and latterly the Parliamentary Labour group, of following the lead of the Irish nationalist party with its capitalist leadership on all questions relative to Ireland, to the detriment of the claims of Irish socialist and labour opinion. George Barnes, leader of the Parliamentary Labour group stated this rationale thus;

> We of the Labour Party favour the whole bill [i.e. without the partition measures] but we take our cue from the Irishmen on the Nationalist benches.[3]
>
> . . . the Nationalists of Ireland have sent men to Parliament, and the Labour men have not. I assume that the Irishmen know their mind and business best, and I take it as expressed in that fact.[4]

For Connolly, still burdened by a sense of the industrial betrayal of the Dublin transport workers by British labour, this new betrayal of Irish political interests over partition served further to alienate him from the British movement. Behind Barnes's legalistic formula lay the electoral calculations for getting in the Irish working-class vote in Britain. In terms of retaining that critical allegiance, the British Labour Party really had little room for manoeuvre outside the demonstrable actions of the Irish Parliamentary Party. Connolly appealed to the Labour Party to stand out for the whole bill and to vote against it if any exclusion were attempted, simply in its own electoral interests. He stressed that,

> Labour men in and out of Ireland have often declared that if Home Rule were wanted for no other purpose, it was necessary in order to allow of the solidifying of the Labour vote in Great Britain, and the rescue of the Irish voters in that country from their thraldom to the Liberal caucus. [And now] . . . the Home Rule question as far as Ulster is concerned, may be indefinitely prolonged and kept alive as an issue to divide and disrupt the Labour vote in Great Britain.[5]

He bluntly told George Barnes and his parliamentary colleagues that – whatever the position of the nationalists might be – from the point of view of organised Labour in Ireland, '. . . we would much rather see the Home Rule bill defeated than see it carried with Ulster, or any part of Ulster, left out'.[6]

And yet Connolly was not in the least surprised by Barnes's attitude. It came as further vindication of his own long-standing contention that, because of the peculiar backwardness of the Irish movement, it required an autonomous organisation of its own and could not be regarded simply as a British appendage. Indeed, as regards revolutionary impetus, Connolly made it clear that Irish backwardness might be a national advantage. On these lines, he personally had, ' . . . fought for the separate political organisation of the Irish workers, and for the separate economic and industrial organisation of the Irish workers on a more revolutionary basis than was usual in England and Scotland'.[7]

Connolly added that in face of the partition proposal – and of its own implied dismemberment by the measure – the Irish labour movement's practice would become increasingly incomprehensible to the British Labour leadership.

If partition threatened physically to divide the Irish workers' movement, it presaged an even deeper theoretical chasm between the principled standpoints of Irish and British socialism. In ISRP policy statements before the turn of the century, and notably in *Erin's Hope*, Connolly had tried to disabuse British socialists of their over-sanguine confidence in the innate 'progressiveness' of Home Rule *per se* for the cause of labour in Ireland. It was this same Liberal/radical-type reasoning on the issue of the imperialist connection between Ireland and the British state which now allowed Labour politicians at Westminster to follow the nationalist lead on partition. Connolly's remarks on the revolutionary value of Irish backwardness are very instructive. The relatively underdeveloped nature of Irish capitalism and hence of the Irish labour movement itself, compared with metropolitan British conditions, had facilitated a correspondingly more revolutionary and class-conscious organisational form in Ireland, i.e. the national OBU. The notion that revolutionary consciousness can develop in the colonial peripheries of the capitalist powers is of course the cornerstone of the Leninist theory of imperialism as the ultimate stage of capitalist development: it was in this sense that Lenin advanced his programme of an international 'proletarian' revolt through the national struggles of subject colonial peoples against European imperial powers. Connolly saw the Irish national struggle against British imperialism in terms very similar to Lenin's schema. While the British government remained committed in principle to a grant of self-determination (no matter how limited in the initial form) to the whole of Ireland, the Irish working-class movement might pursue its class struggle within the new political arrangement. Because Ireland was a dependent unit within the British imperial structure, the labour movement had to be freed from the incubus of unrealised national aspiration in order to mobilise democratic support for the socialist goal. Hence:

> The cause of labour is the cause of Ireland, the cause of Ireland is the cause of labour. They cannot be dissevered. Ireland seeks freedom. Labour seeks that an Ireland free should be the sole mistress of her own destiny, supreme owner of all material things within and upon her soil. Labour seeks to make the free Irish nation the guardian of the interests of the people of Ireland, and to secure that end would vest in that free Irish nation all property rights against the claims of the individual, with the end in view that the individual may be enriched by the nation, and not by the spoiling of his fellows.[8]

The British Labour leadership failed to see that partition would make it impossible in principle for the revolutionary Irish labour movement thus to evolve its independent practice beyond the nationalist incubus. Partition asserted the principle that Ireland was two 'nations' and not one: it sought to establish two antagonistic sub-states, loyalist and nationalist, each of which would be held in economic trust for the empire by local comprador classes, the Orange and Home Rule bourgeois establishments. Against such a reactionary scheme, even such a highly radical class-conscious movement as had emerged under the conditions of Irish backwardness, would be helpless. Above all, partition was a forced response to the threat of the use of armed force on the part of the Ulster loyalists. No matter what the bourgeois nationalist leadership might be induced to accept, Connolly was clear that the labour movement would have to be *coerced* into acquiescence, so high were the stakes. It was equally clear that Connolly's Citizen Army force would be mobilised to resist all attempts to impose partition, either by the regular forces of the crown or by the irregular volunteer force of the Ulster 'provisional government'. From Connolly's point of view, the capitulation of the elected government to the Ulster irregulars in the form of the partition scheme, made a pre-emptive counter-strike against it by the military arms of the nationalist and labour movements inevitable.

What Connolly himself described as the 'natural alliance' between Nationalists and Labour[9] over the partition issue was firmly cemented by the outbreak of world war in the first week of August 1914. The coming of war decided Connolly on an unequivocal path to insurrection and from that time until the actual outbreak of the Easter Rising in 1916, it was Connolly who forced the pace upon his slower moving nationalist allies. In September 1914 Connolly made contact with the leadership of the clandestine IRB and negotiations were begun with a view to preparing an Irish military insurrection with German aid.[10] The IRB had had much success in penetrating the structure of the Irish Volunteers and it was this capacity, together with proposed musters of the Citizen Army on which these plans depended. Connolly hoped that on the European continent, a general transport strike supplemented by mass civil disobedience, sabotage of communication facilities, paralysis of cities through the erection of defended barricades and mutiny in the ranks of the armed forces would be organised by the socialist movement and cripple the war effort of the separate nations. None of these eventualities he thought, even should civil conflict ensue, could lead to as great a loss of working-class lives as would mass participation in the conscript armies of the belligerent powers. For Connolly, nothing could compare with the total abomination of the horrors of this imperialist war:

> . . . the most fearful crime of the centuries. In it, the working class are to be sacrificed that a small clique of rulers and armament makers may sate their lust for power and their greed for wealth. Nations are to be obliterated, progress stopped and international hatreds erected into deities to be worshipped.[11]

In general, British socialist and labour leaders came out in support of the national war effort, arguing their case in terms of the defence of civilised values, of the norms of international law and that the very enormity of the conflict would ensure its being the last. Repudiating this kind of thinking, Connolly scoffed:

> . . . we cannot draw upon the future for a draft to pay our present duties. There is no moratorium to postpone the payment of the debt the socialists owe to the cause; it can only be paid now. Paid it may be in martyrdom, but a few hundred such martyrdoms would be but a small price to pay to avert the slaughter of hundreds of thousands.[12]

Connolly's internationalist stand on the war issue was substantially similar to that of Lenin. Just as Connolly repudiated the notion that socialists might suspend their commitment to class struggle in the interest of defending the homeland,[13] Lenin reminded the leaders of European socialism that this same notion utterly contradicted Marx's own view – first adumbrated by Clausewitz – that war should be regarded as the continuation of all forms of politics by other (i.e. violent) means: hence the prosecution of the class struggle was as urgent a socialist commitment in time of war as in time of peace; notions that it might be suspended for the duration of hostilities in deference to other values, were theoretically nonsensical.[14] For Lenin, such 'social-chauvinism', as he termed it, was a natural function of the reformist trends within social democracy.[15] Connolly saw the same weaknesses in unreservedly syndicalist terms, and stressed the importance of the crippling divorce between the industrial and political wings of the working-class movement in the belligerent countries. The syndicalist organisational schema – the vote backed by a strong class-conscious economic organisation – could alone guarantee the workers both a structural base upon which to build the post-capitalist socialist commonwealth *and* a flexible weapon with which to meet every exigency – war included – which might arise during the repressive period of capitalism's death throes.[16] In regard to the situation within the British Isles, it was the failure of the ITWU's struggle against the Dublin employers in 1913 which had signalled the weakness of syndicalist forces: moreover, that very backwardness of the Irish labour movement which had entailed an extraordinary revolutionary basis for its organisation, meant that it now had special obligations in the wartime crisis. Connolly was at this time clearly convinced that these obligations could be discharged only in insurrectionary terms.

Connolly's commitment to the principle of physical force in 1914 stands in formal contradiction to the democratic-syndicalist approach he had evolved after almost a quarter-century's work in the social democratic movement. Although, from the time of the Boer war, Connolly felt unable to *rule out* in principle the use of force as a last resort in the proletarian revolution, his syndicalist ideology – based upon American experience – held that the operation of the revolutionary industrial union structure alone (through imposition of total economic paralysis) would be sufficient *quietus* should the capitalist regime itself resort to coercive violence in its last days. However, the validity of this industrial unionist programme was severely challenged in 1914, first by the peculiarities and 'backwardness' of the Irish situation and, secondly in a more general way by the outbreak of world war.

The Irish partition proposal by the Asquith government involved a hitherto *unimaginable* surrender of jurisdiction in the face of unconstitutional force, on the part of the bourgeois state.

The manifest inability of the state to enforce its will signalled a radical breakdown of the liberal polity and meant that such enforcement could only be assumed by 'progressive' (labour and nationalist) irregular forces. Significantly enough, and responding to this political breakdown pathology, it was in connection with the government's failure to deal with the Ulster Volunteers that Connolly first considered armed resistance. The outbreak of imperialist world war exacerbated this breakdown pathology, and the situation was further worsened and complicated by the total failure of international socialism to mount any effective effort to end hostilities. Such a cataclysmic end to the bourgeois-capitalist world had long been anticipated by social democrats, but the utter helplessness of their own organisations in the face of it had not. Although the peculiar weakness of the Irish OBU precluded a serious anti-war strike in Ireland in the summer of 1914, it quickly became evident that even the prestigious socialist parties and unions of France and Germany were equally impotent. As each of the belligerent powers prepared themselves for prolonged hostilities, constitutional freedoms vital both to the conduct of socialist propaganda and to the welfare of workers on the job began systematically to disappear, all in the interest of a more effective war effort. As Connolly contemplated the awesome imponderable of where the liberal state breakdown might lead under the strains of modern total war, the loss or suspension of rights won by labour under the liberal constitution and the practical constraints on party and union activity, he turned to the Citizen Army as the one remaining vehicle capable of genuine class-conscious action. Commander of Europe's first 'red army' gradually became his prime role.

This role was confirmed as wartime legislation assumed an increasingly repressive logic. The wide latitude of powers given military and police authorities under the Defence of the Realm Acts – which included suspension of trial by jury, powers of search without warrant and penalties of imprisonment or deportation for activities calculated to undermine the war effort in any way – severely hampered left-wing and labour activists and publicists throughout the United Kingdom. A rigorous censorship of both speech and print was enforced by specially created 'Competent Military Authorities', and the system thus imposed upon the civilian population amounted to little short of martial law. On the industrial front, the Munitions of War Act of 1915 introduced a new labour code which suspended many hard-won trade union rights. It contained provisions for the compulsory arbitration of trades disputes, suspension of all trades practices (including apprenticeship standards, job demarcation and the right of trade union officials to recruit and represent their own members) together with a 'leaving certificate' system to enforce greater discipline. This last provision made it mandatory for workers employed on munitions work to gain their employers' permission if they wished to change jobs. In Ireland, the suspension of such civil and industrial liberties caused particularly acute problems. Whereas British trade unions had long been recognised, and their co-operation was sought regarding the operation of the new labour code, less well-established Irish unions such as the ITWU were now threatened with extinction. The Dublin lock-out of 1913-14 had been fought over the precise issue of union recognition by the transport employers. Having failed to destroy the Irish OBU in peacetime, such employers attempted to make use of the wartime labour code to dismiss union members (ostensibly for enlistment in the forces) and replace them with female or 'scab' labour. Many Irish unions – the ITWU in particular – faced obliteration through the operation of such informal, 'economic conscription'.

While in Great Britain it was almost exclusively the labour and socialist movement which found its freedoms thus constrained by the wartime legislation, in Ireland the nationalist movement suffered equal constraint and harassment. As regards attitudes to the imperial war effort, recruitment, conscription and the like, nationalist publicists and speakers were as disabled from expressing their views freely as was Connolly himself. Nationalist journals and meetings were suppressed, proclaimed and generally harassed with equal frequency and severity as their labour counterparts. In the period December 1914–April 1916, Connolly had various journals successively suppressed by the authorities: *The Irish Worker, Irish Work, The Worker* and *The Workers' Republic* were all ITWU organs brought out as separate publications after their predecessors had been suppressed. On the nationalist side, the publication of *Sinn Féin. Irish Freedom,*

Eire – Ireland and the *Gael* was similarly disrupted in the same period. Protesting against the loss of freedoms of speech, publication, association and demonstration, Connolly spoke as much for the nationalists as for labour when he declaimed;

> The liberty of public meeting is . . . rapidly becoming a thing of the past in Ireland, as far as it is or may be used for the criticism of the activities of the government or its functionaries; and yet it is this very right of the subject to criticise the governing bodies which is the very essence of freedom in a constitutionally governed country. Without the freedom of the press and the right of public meeting there is no citizenship; there are only the relations of subject and rulers, of slaves and slave-drivers . . . The press criticisms are subject to the judgment of the readers; the public meeting stands or falls with the justice of its cause. To allow either to be judged or punished by those against whom they are directed, is to abolish all constitutional guarantees and to establish the naked rule of force . . .[17]

In this worsening climate, the occurrence of some commemorative patriot ceremonies gave Connolly an opportunity to prepare the Irish working class psychologically for the near certainty of insurrection. In June 1915, the Fenian veteran O'Donovan Rossa died in New York and his body was repatriated from the USA for interment in Irish soil. A lying-in-state organised in late July at the City Hall, Dublin, and the funeral in Glasnevin on 1 August were occasions for massive devotional demonstrations by radical nationalist forces. P. H. Pearse delivered a graveside oration which must be numbered among the most passionate – and verbose – expressions of the romantic nationalism of that generation. The peculiar messianic martyrdom-*cum*-Gaelic heroism which comprised the christian-pagan romantic complexity of intellectuals such as Pearse, was also evident in Connolly's response to Rossa. In a sustained mystical vein, Connolly observed in the 7 August issue of his *Workers' Republic*:

> . . . the fight in Ireland has been one for the soul of a race –

> that Irish race which with seven centuries of defeat behind it still battled for the sanctity of its dwelling place . . . medieval legends tell us how in the critical moments of the struggle of an army, or the travail of a nation, some angel or deliverer was sent from above to save those favoured by the Most High. To many people today it seems that the funeral of O'Donovan Rossa came to Ireland in such a moment of national agony – came on such a mission of divine uplifting and deliverance. The mists, the doubts, the corruption and poisons, the distrust and the treacheries, were blown away, and the true men and women of Ireland saw with pleasure the rally of the nation to the olden ideas . . .

The anniversaries in November of three Fenians executed for the killing of a Manchester policeman in September 1867 during an attempt to free two comrades from custody, allowed Connolly further scope to argue for direct action. Stressing the attempt was carried out despite all practical arguments against its success, Connolly described it in the 21 November issue of the *Workers' Republic* as a sacrifice made ' . . . that the right of their small nationality to independence might be attested by their blood . . . that some day an Irish Republic might live'.

These expressions of the virtue of a cleansing and redeeming self-sacrifice for the soul of the nation clearly show the grounds for Connolly's co-operation with romantic nationalists of Pearse's stamp. They also show how Connolly's tactical options had been narrowed to the insurrectionary line by the 'corruption . . . poisons . . . and treacheries' in the body politic of contemporary Ireland: the shelving of Home Rule for the duration of hostilities; the apparent inevitability of some kind of partition of the country when it would eventually be enacted; the resultant ethno-religious polarisation within the Irish working class; the erosion of civil and trades liberties by the warfare state; the near dismemberment of the ITWU.

Connolly had assumed full command of the Citizen Army in October 1914, inheriting this function – along with the general secretaryship of the ITWU and the editorship of the union paper the *Irish Worker* – from Jim Larkin who left at that time for the USA. The force was no longer the makeshift body of unarmed men which had attempted to ward off police attacks at the height of the Dublin lock-out. In March, mainly on the initiative of its secretary Sean O'Casey, it had been enlarged and reformed, membership being opened to all trade unionists willing to arm in the defence of a united Ireland and to enforce the right of the people to ' . . . the ownership of Ireland, moral and material'. Recruiting for the force had also taken an upward trend with the manifesto issued the same month by the Irish TUC urging workers to assert their right to arm in defence of economic freedom. As reorganised by O'Casey, the army became something of a mass movement, rivalling the Volunteers in conception at least, and a degree of recruiting competition developed between the two organisations. O'Casey's hopes that the force would develop into a mass labour para-military body were never realised. When the Irish parliamentary leader John Redmond imposed his own nominees on the Volunteer executive (men from the Dublin capitalist class whom the ITWU had bitterly fought only the previous year), O'Casey resigned over the issue of the close association between the Citizen and Volunteer forces. By the time of Connolly's arrival to take command at Liberty Hall in October the Volunteer movement had split, fully nine-tenths of its membership having followed Redmond's lead in pledging Irish nationalist support for the British war effort. As Citizen Army commander, Connolly sought allies among the IRB-dominated Volunteer rump for his design to mount an insurrectionary counter-strike against the imperialist war machine.

Connolly swiftly began a radically new regime of Citizen Army activity. Appointing trusted officers, he instituted serious and regular weapons training, munitions manufacture, tactical study and even attempted to make automatic weaponry. The Citizen force was shaped to his immediate purpose: a compact, well-trained, *reliably disciplined* body ready to answer their commander's mobilisation call whenever necessary and without question. Connolly's reform actually reduced the size of the force from several hundreds to about two hundred men: however it was a force more in keeping with the number of weapons available to arm it and the reduction in numbers was more than offset by greater discipline and *esprit*. As Connolly developed the

Citizen Army from a semi-recreational body marching and parading in symbolic opposition to partition into a serious and formidable military unit, friction arose between him and some of the more straightforward trade unionists in the ITWU. Diplomacy and tact were required on more than one occasion to soothe trade unionist anxieties and apprehensions about the Citizen armourers who worked and prepared in the bowels of Liberty Hall. If Connolly's republican and militarist line did not enjoy full support within the advanced nationalist ITWU, it was even less representative of organised labour generally: the Irish labour movement then contained every possible variation of opinion from loyalism to republican separatism and from constitutional to direct action policy preferences.

Connolly's conspiratorial allies in the IRB were in a similar minority position within the Irish Volunteer structure, with the added difficulty of a confused chain of command. Even after the Redmondite split, the secret brotherhood remained a clandestine minority within the nationalist para-military organisation, albeit one with its own sworn adherents at every key point in the command structure. The Volunteer commitment had been mobilisation to oppose partition and act as an extra-parliamentary lobby force in support of Home Rule before the outbreak of war: with hostilities ongoing, the general policy of the force was to await a European truce before taking action to assert Ireland's claims to independence, or, to take defensive action should the authorities attempt to disarm them or enforce conscription or in the (unlikely) event of a German landing in force. The IRB position was one of preparing for an armed insurrection at the earliest opportune moment while the British government was preoccupied with the conduct of the war and to use its own placemen within the Volunteer structure as a lever to commit that entire body to offensive action. While the IRB sought to enforce a clandestine authority of its own in parallel to that of Volunteer Chief-of-Staff Eoin MacNeill, it was handicapped by its own will for secrecy. During the course of 1915 a 'military council' was established by the IRB to plan and co-ordinate its plans for insurrection. This group eventually included Tom Clarke and Sean MacDermott (the two most powerful men in the brotherhood) together with P. H. Pearse, Eamonn Ceannt and

Joseph Plunkett. The very existence of the military council was kept a guarded secret even from the general membership of the IRB. In Dublin, where communication between this secret council and IRB commanders of city Volunteer units could remain close, there was no command problem. In the provinces, Volunteer officers of IRB membership were unaware that such a supreme brotherhood authority existed distinct from the formal authority of Volunteer headquarters staff. This ignorance – a function of the way in which MacDermott and Clarke personally operated and controlled the brotherhood – was a recipe for provincial confusion should the military council's designs at any time be detected and opposed by Volunteer headquarters staff.

Throughout 1915 Connolly and the IRB leaders – Tom Clarke, Sean MacDermott and P. H. Pearse – worked to improve the training and efficiency of the Citizen Army and the Volunteers. A plan was evolved for an insurrection in Dublin in the autumn of 1915, to be supported by a mobilisation of Volunteers in the provinces who would be equipped with arms landed by a German ship on the Kerry coast. The tasks of the provincial forces remained vague, amounting to little more than diversionary moves to relieve the pressure on the mainforce in Dublin. The Dublin plan consisted in the establishment of insurgent garrisons at selected strongpoints in the inner city and thereafter sustaining the newly proclaimed Irish Republic for as long as the inevitable assaults of the British forces could be resisted. When the position seemed doubtful with regard to the German arms supplies, the IRB decided on a postponement and it was at this time, during the final months of 1915, that relations between Connolly and the secret brotherhood became strained. Impatient at the delay and fearful that the government might pre-empt the entire enterprise by wholesale arrests of nationalist and labour leaders, Connolly then began to doubt the seriousness of the IRB's commitment to armed rebellion. For their part, the IRB feared that Connolly might himself initiate a premature and disastrous unilateral mobilisation of the Citizen Army force before their own organisation was fully prepared. In January 1916, Connolly and the IRB came to an agreement for an armed rising to be staged in Easter week of that year. The same defensive plan for Dublin was adhered to and the German arms shipment was scheduled to be landed in Kerry in the last week in April. It was hoped that the insurgent 'Army of the Irish Republic' might hold out until the end of the European war (expected at an early date) and thus gain separate recognition at the Peace Conference as a sovereign ally of Germany. That same month, Connolly justified his programme of action in a statement whose basic syndicalist content was unequivocal.[18]

> Our programme in time of Peace was to gather into Irish hands in Irish trade unions the control of all the forces of production and distribution in Ireland . . . our ends should be secured 'peacefully if possible, forcibly if necessary' . . . Thus we strove to make Labour in Ireland organised – and revolutionary.

Referring to the nationalist and class spirit of the ITWU he said, 'We have succeeded in creating an organisation that will willingly do more for Ireland than any trade union in the world has attempted to do for its national government.'

He then made it clear that – given the war situation – the only difference of strategy was that the OBU was now held in readiness to support the *military arm* of the workers' and nationalist movement, military action having become the natural function of politics in the changed situation of general war. Connolly averred that had the nationalist leadership in general supported the OBU when it was attacked and undermined by the Dublin employers in 1913,[19] it would now be in a stronger position thus to support the military arm:

> Had we been able to carry out all of our plans, as such an Irish organisation of labour alone could carry them out, we could at a word have created all the conditions necessary to the striking of a successful blow whenever the military arm of Ireland wished to move.

Just as the OBU was held in readiness in peacetime to enforce the socialist decision of the ballot by means of a general stoppage of work; so, in time of war insurrection would be facilitated by widespread strike action, especially of workers employed in the transport and communications fields.

In the event, the Irish revolution, as begun in the Easter

Week Rising on Monday, 24 April 1916, could not correspond to this formula of insurrection – *cum* – national general strike. The ITWU had been weakened by the 1913 lock-out and by the operation of economic conscription beyond all capacity for calling a serious and widespread stoppage of work. At the eleventh hour Eoin MacNeill had become aware of the insurrectionary designs of his IRB subordinates and had formally cancelled the Easter weekend manoeuvres upon which the insurgent leaders had been relying for a mobilisation of full Volunteer strength. This countermanding instruction caused more confusion and paralysis among volunteers in the provinces than in the city itself, although it did delay the commencement of hostilities for 24 hours. The chief effect of the order was positive for the insurgents since it allayed the fears of the Dublin Castle authorities who were at the time considering mass arrests of leading activists in the para-military nationalist movements. MacNeill's action may have resulted in some reductions in the strength of the units deployed in Dublin on the Easter Monday, but it should be recalled that there was ample time and opportunity for absent soldiers (on both sides) who wished to, to rejoin their units during the first day or two of the rising: many did so. The commanders of the insurgent battalions made sure to give their men advance warning of the seriousness of the intended conflict, and this doubtless led to many individual decisions not to muster on the actual day.[20]

Connolly and his IRB associates knowingly went out that Easter Monday to meet inevitable defeat and death at the hands of British imperial power. For the IRB it was a move made in the hope that their martyrdom would prove inspirational for the future of the Irish cause: Connolly was self-consciously paying his debt to the socialist cause; going to his duty as a socialist and internationalist amidst the holocaust of total war. The Republic was proclaimed from the steps of the General Post Office, and the Army of the Republic – of which Connolly was named commanding general – awaited the inevitable onslaught. For almost a week these few hundred riflemen held out against overwhelming British forces equipped with superior automatic weaponry and assisted by artillery and armoured vehicles. After five days of street fighting, and with the headquarters unit of the republican army burned and shelled out of its GPO stronghold, the Provisional Government of the Republic ordered an unconditional capitulation. Within 24 hours all insurgent units had complied and had laid down their arms. Following courts-martial, the members of the provisional government – including Connolly who had been badly wounded in the fighting – were summarily executed together with most of their subordinate commanders.

Connolly made no defence at the court-martial held at his hospital bedside, save a dignified denial of the rather spurious charge of needlessly exposing to fire certain British prisoners captured by the republicans. His last statement is one of a man without personal doubts or recriminations and who expected and demanded no clemency.[21] At this point he expressed concern about the reactions of British socialists to his involvement in the insurrection. Expecting little real understanding from anglo-marxists, it was then that he made his celebrated comment, '. . . they will all forget I am an Irishman'.[22] Connolly's comment should be seen in the context of the work he had done to establish the theoretical and organisational basis for a class-concious and independent working-class movement in Ireland. As an Irishman in the international socialist movement – but particularly within the English-speaking movement – he had attempted to pursue an Irish road to socialism. If this pursuit had led him to a position of relative isolation within the working-class movement in Ireland itself, it had put him beyond the comprehension of his erstwhile comrades in Britain and the USA. His evolution toward an insurrectionary standpoint provoked baffled criticism from these reformist quarters, the British ILP even going to the lengths of condemning the Rising as a form of militarism.[23] It was logical enough that constitutionalists could have no sympathy for any kind of practice which failed to respect the strict constraints of the bourgeois state form. Lenin himself, although seemingly unaware of just how sophisticated a marxist had played such a leading role in the rebellion, hailed it as a genuine revolutionary event, if rather 'premature'. Such struggles among the oppressed nations of Europe, he wrote, would greatly sharpen the emergent revolutionary crisis for European imperialism as the war progressed.[24]

As a choice of revolutionary policy, Connolly's insurrectionary commitment in the 1914-16 period can be seen to have a principled base in many of his earlier stands on important issues. It was a not unprecedented response to war and also an extra-constitutional response to the unconstitutional armed manoeuvrings of the Unionist partitionists in Ulster. It was a function of his alliance with the radical forces of romantic nationalism against the bankrupt notion of a putative Irish liberal state promoted by the Home Rule party – a position he maintained from the time of his arrival in Dublin in 1896. It was also a commitment made possible by his post-De Leonite syndicalist ideology which asserted a standpoint beyond parliamentary politics and constitutional form: a class standpoint based upon the marxist principle of the state *as a function* of the class factor and not – as the reformists believed – a reality independent of it. And, in the final analysis, Connolly possessed the immense physical and mental courage to put life itself second to the dictates of his conscience and intellect.

4. Historiography and Scientific Materialism

At the most general level of principle, Connolly's marxist philosophy was based upon tenets which were highly unorthodox in nature. However his unorthodoxy should be viewed as a logical outcome of the highly problematic nature of 'orthodox marxism' as a system, rather than as some kind of individual eccentricity. Writing history was the chief intellectual means through which Connolly addressed and attempted to overcome the problems of principle implicit in the orthodox doctrine; but before assessing his particular achievement in this regard, some consideration must be given to the more general intellectual heritage of the marxist movement.

As the official doctrine of the international socialist movement, 'marxism' was a fusion of materialist historiography and sociological science, but, as the nineteenth century drew toward its close, the scientific element became predominant. Following the predictive and determinist logic of scientific method, orthodox marxism viewed history as the record of social change forced along by inexorable economic factors: historical explanation was a function of general 'laws' of development, analagous to the empirically determined laws of experimental science. However, this doctrine was regarded by the orthodox as more than simply the science of history or of social development. It appeared as the ultimate form of science itself; the paradigm for scientific investigation of the totality of both the human and natural worlds. Later dubbed 'dialectical materialism', the method became a metaphysical overview capable of explaining the natural phenomena investigated by empirical science as well as the variables of human behaviour and belief observable over the timespan of history.

A brief look at the origins of the marxist theory brings out the problematic nature of its later dependence upon positive scientific method. When Marx first undertook to invert the logic of the Hegelian system, to establish a material, historically causal basis for the dialectical method in place of Hegel's idealist mode, he had no intention of dispensing with its speculative content. On the contrary, the whole point of dialectical method was the value of speculative insight gained thereby and Marx's self-conscious starting point – with Hegel's logic – was also a rejection of the alternative approach of positive science. Technically, Marx's new 'historical materialism' drew attention to the importance of material elements as historical *factors* (social class, the forces of production and so on). These were, in effect, empirical tools for the equipment of historical science, but were not intended for use in a merely positive or objective fashion. Methodologically, the *aim* of this approach was the demonstration of the marxist metaphysic of 'practice' – a speculative notion of human nature which, if not Hegelian in origin, was based in Hegel's concept of mind. According to the idea of practice, man is in essence the free creator of both his world and his own consciousness. History, the record of human practice, Marx regarded as nothing less than the unfolding self-realisation through time of the unity of consciousness and its objects. Hence, history would demonstrate the speculative principle of the union of theory and practice. The science of historical materialism had as its purpose the demonstration of this unfolding historical process by establishing logical connections between social and economic factors on the one hand and intellectual developments on the other.

Thus formulated, materialist method was intended to serve the revolutionary interest of the proletariat, the class designated the inheritor of classical German philosophy (idealism).[1] The later marxist orthodoxy however, in its pursuit of the scientific, assumed a relativist standpoint on all normative questions, reducing intellectual phenomena to 'reflections' of material factors. This development effectually reduced the proletarian intellectual inheritance to an empirical super-positivism devoid of normative and value content. As a counter to this orthodox standpoint, the revisionist marxists of Germany and Austria asserted the compatibility of marxist materialism with Kantian ethics as a defence of normative values which were universal and nonrelative.[2] This Kantian revival was by implication an attempt to restore the lost inheritance of German idealism and the entire christian intellectual tradition upon which it rested. In his own fashion, James Connolly attempted to bridge the same conceptual gap between scientific determinism and the christian intellectual heritage. For him, the christian tradition of Irish Catholicism, together with the (more romantically perceived) practice of Irish Gaeldom, remained sources of spiritual and ethical values which determinist science could not logically comprehend or accommodate in its own terms.

For Connolly, the urgency of tackling the problem of the relationship between materialist science and questions of value led naturally toward an active involvement in historiography. If marxist theory generally had achieved a principled 'union of theory and practice', Connolly's historiography aimed in similar fashion to demonstrate how science and value might be united within one historical vision. Connolly's attempt to comprehend the totality of the Irish experience was also an attempt to comprehend empirical and normative kinds of thinking. Connolly held that the history of the Irish people was also the history of that people's consciousness: historiography was charged with the task of describing the enduring nature of the normative values of Gaeldom and Irish christianity through time, no less than with an empirical demonstration of the determining role of material factors in Irish history.

This standpoint emerged as a mature commitment of Connolly's later years and was based on a consistent intellectual struggle lasting more than two decades. Very broadly, there were three phases to this evolutionary struggle. As a young activist in his native city of Edinburgh in the early 1890s, he first took a principled stand against all who sought to identify socialism with free thought and hostility to moral standards. At a later period, around the turn of the century, Connolly adopted an ultra-left 'purist' approach both in theory and method, associating himself closely with the American Socialist Labor Party and its leader Daniel De Leon. Essentially a move to dissociate the marxist party from 'class unconscious' bodies working within the bourgeois economic and political system (i.e. conventional trade unions and reformist 'labour' parties), Connolly's new standpoint nonetheless remained firmly committed to an assertion of non-relative values. It was at this time that he spoke out most strongly against comrades (De Leon included) of the ultramaterialist stamp who tended to conflate marxist principle with irreligion and amorality. Simultaneously, Connolly also made his first attempt to write serious scholarly history. Finally, after his return to Ireland from the USA in 1910, Connolly's major work, *Labour in Irish History* appeared. This ambitious historiographical attempt to comprehend the experience, consciousness and values of the Irish people, Connolly offered as a contribution to the nativist cultural renaissance then flourishing in Ireland.

When Connolly joined the social democratic movement in Edinburgh early in 1890, he entered what was then a loosely organised federative movement with small groups in provincial centres affiliated to the main centre of activity in London.[3] Founded in the preceding decade as a direct response to Marx's critique of bourgeois society and economics as outlined in the first volume of *Capital*, the movement had many roots besides marxist materialism. Contemporary positive sociology was held in great esteem by leading British socialists, notably the work of Lewis Morgan whose *Ancient Society* ran the marxist classics a close second in popularity within the movement. British socialism also drew heavily on the secular tradition in politics inherited from the Bradlaugh movement of the previous generation and also from the evangelical radicalism evident in both the established churches and in non-conformist denominations. It would be entirely proper to describe British social democracy at this time as a movement of 'advanced democratic' character upon which a marxist programme had been grafted.

Within this somewhat diffuse theoretical and organisational situation, the Edinburgh group which Connolly joined – the 'Scottish Socialist Federation' – insisted in its constitution that its members ' . . . acknowledge Truth, Justice and Morality as the basis for their behaviour among themselves and towards all their fellow men'.[4] This principled commitment to normative values beyond an essentialist materialism produced some criticism of the SSF within the movement at large from comrades of a more determinist marxist stamp. The SSF's stand on the matter resulted from its background linked to an evangelical radicalism of the presbyterian type. One of its foremost members, and the tutor of its study classes for the instruction of young members (Connolly himself included) was the Rev. Dr John Glasse, Minister of the Old Greyfriars kirk. A close friend of the socialist leader William Morris, John Glasse enjoined his fellow churchmen to resolve ' . . . in the spirit of the prophets and of Jesus, to work along with the socialists in breaking every yoke and letting the oppressed go free'.[5] John Glasse regarded the tendencies toward doctrinaire determinism within the socialist movement as highly self-destructive. However, he was disposed toward optimism in the final analysis:

> The socialists will, like the Christians, refuse to identify themselves with self-satisfied and dogmatic cliques . . . and [will] realise an institution that in catholicity can only be compared with the Romish church.[6]

From his presbyterian mentor, Connolly learned in thorough detail how the first volume of *Capital* had (to use one of John Glasse's favourite remarks) elevated socialism from the realm of the artificial and utopian to that of academic science. As a member himself of the 'Romish church', Connolly also received from the Rev. comrade an inspirational notion of how socialism should come to embody in its own practice the universal values of the christian tradition. It was on this basis that the young Connolly denied in public on at least two occasions, that socialism was hostile to the sacrament of marriage. The materialist approach of some leading socialists – among them some of the pioneer feminists – disposed them to view marriage as a vehicle of bourgeois oppression which would wither away under socialism. In January 1896, Connolly chided one of Dr Glasse's fellow clergymen for taking this to be the principled view of socialism and using it as a basis for an anti-marxist lecture.[7] The following month he crossed swords with the nationally known socialist feminist Edith Lanchester on the same 'free love' issue. Introducing her to an Edinburgh public meeting, he reminded the audience that, ' . . . socialism had no connection with speculations on family life and was nowise responsible for the opinions of individual socialists on that subject'.[8]

The ideological fluidity of the left in Britain – which nourished complex standpoints such as that of the Edinburgh SSF – gradually hardened as the 'nineties progressed. These were the years of rapid growth of the new parliamentary Independent Labour Party, an organisation which absorbed the energies of the evangelical 'christian socialist' tradition. Meanwhile, marxist theory was accommodated to the freethinking-secularist tradition within the smaller Social Democratic Federation, with which the old SSF fused in 1895. Connolly unhesitatingly chose the marxist road both in Edinburgh and later in Dublin when he organised the Socialist Republican Party in May 1896.[9] As the turn of the century approached, pressures within the newly 'clarified' marxist movement to conform to the determinist position steadily mounted.

Such pressures assumed a trans-atlantic dimension when, in the late 'nineties, Connolly joined with Daniel De Leon of the American Socialist Labor Party to criticise the political policies of the British SDF leadership. Mainly as a result of this criticism of the SDF's 'opportunism' (co-operation with 'class-unconscious' reformist organisations such as trade unions and the ILP) a breakaway British SLP was founded in 1903 with Connolly as its national organiser. The new party was modelled on what the British dissidents considered to be the correct political attitude of the American party: the problem of determinism remained however and in a much more self-conscious form. Close though he might be in sympathy with the political stand of this ultra-sectarian party, Connolly soon found that philosophically, he was seriously at odds with its total determinist standpoint on matters of value.

Connolly had briefly visited the USA in the fall of 1902 on a lecture tour for the SLP. With some first-hand experience of marxist practice on both sides of the Atlantic, he then drew attention to some general conceptual shortcomings within the English-speaking movement as a whole. In the British De Leonite paper he complained;

> . . . we find imported into our movement . . . a whole host

of theories of political action, tactics and strategy which are foreign to our principles and destructive of our class spirit . . . [i.e.] . . . The sneaking fondness for any man who 'talks physical force' even when he does it to cloak semi-reactionary principles . . . the vague but harmful belief that irreligion is necessarily linked with social revolution and religious orthodoxy with capitalism: the tendency to rush off into all manner of speculations about the future, and the desire to exclude all who do not agree with the speculation upon the tendency resultant from the economic change.[10]

Connolly deplored what he regarded as the iconoclastic destructiveness of the determinist world view and the sympathy for physical force as some kind of revolutionary 'principle' associated with it. He forthrightly characterised this kind of thinking as 'our baneful inheritance from the first French Revolution'.[11] This statement is a reproach against the intellectual bankruptcy of determinist materialism even to understand the nature of religious faith as a social factor – let alone as an important value concept. It is also a sensitive *caveat* against allowing the predictive empirical method to overstep its proper subject matter (i.e. the *course* of economic and material change) to the point of predetermining the details of all spiritual, ethical and intellectual changes which might result. It was a consistent adherence to this principle which, after Connolly's removal to New York in 1903, brought him into direct ideological collision with the austere Daniel De Leon.

The occasion for the dispute with De Leon was Connolly's article on 'Wages, Marriage and the Church' which appeared in the SLP organ *The Weekly People* on 9 April 1904. It is the value question involved in both the marriage and religious issues which concerns the present argument. In his article Connolly attacked what he saw as unwarranted speculation on moral issues, presented as a logical issue of materialist analysis, in August Bebel's book *Woman under Socialism*. This work, by one of the most renowned figures in the German socialist movement, had recently been translated into English by De Leon himself. Connolly wrote,

The abolition of the capitalist system will undoubtedly

solve the economic side of the woman question, but it will solve that alone. The question of marriage, of divorce, of paternity and of the equality of woman with man are physical and sexual questions, or questions of temperamental affiliation as in marriage and were we living in a socialist rcpublic would still be as hotly contested as they are today.

This limitation of predictive empirical method to the *course* of change only, and to the exclusion of changes in belief or opinion that might result, outraged De Leon. He characterised Connolly's statement as, ' . . . utopian, in that it denies the controlling influence of material conditions upon any and all social institutions'.[12]

In keeping with such determinist thinking, De Leon was also disposed to adopt a crypto-secularist hostility to organised religion in general and to the Roman Catholic faith in particular. Despite the Erfurt ruling of 1891 – adopted as authoritative by the International – which removed the question of religious belief from party practice or policy, De Leon had himself written of the urgency for socialists to take a stand against 'organised churchdom'.[13] As editor of *The People*, he had included in its 19 March issue – without comment – an article by the Belgian socialist leader Emile Vandervelde which appeared to substitute an anti-religious struggle for the class struggle as the prime socialist commitment. Vandervelde combined an apology for bourgeois liberalism with hortatory comments on the value of reformist politics for the workers' struggle; he then suggested that the real enemy of the working class was the Roman Catholic church, and not the capitalist class. The ultimate struggle in his view would be one between the 'Red International' (socialism) and the 'Black', (Catholicism), capitalist institutions being mere transient intermediaries. He wrote:

Justice forbids . . . to reproach English Liberalism as a body with the reactionary complaisance of the right-wing. In France . . . the republican middle class and the radical democracy do not hesitate to accept the help of the social democracy against the Catholic church by enrolling

Millerand in the ministry and electing Jaurès Vice-President of the Chamber of Deputies.

In his article of 9 April, Connolly charged that for Vandervelde, '. . . the great struggle for freedom is but a kind of side show, or perhaps an auxiliary, to the freethinking movement.'

De Leon had printed the Vandervelde article largely, it would appear, because its argument accorded with his own deeply anti-clerical sentiments. To give such public approval to the bizarre perversion of marxist theory it contained is a clear indication of the follies to which the determinist intellect was prone. As a corrective, it is instructive to recall the comments of Karl Kautsky on the theoretical shortcomings of the Belgian socialist leadership. Two years previously he had said of them:

> . . . they have no theory. The eclectic vulgar socialism to which the revisionists would like to reduce marxism is something beyond which they (the Belgians) have not even begun to advance. Proudhon, Schäffle, Marx – it is all one to them: it was always like that . . .[14]

The fact that it was determinist dogmatism in principle which Connolly sought to combat, and not a sense of personally outraged religiosity, is well illustrated by his comments to a Scottish comrade penned a few years later. This statement clearly shows that what was at issue was a matter of general principle and not a question of offended religious sentiment. On his own admission, Connolly had no vestige of conventional faith remaining:

> . . . though I have usually posed as a Catholic, I have not gone to my duty for fifteen years, and I have not the slightest tincture of faith left. I only assumed the Catholic pose to quiz the raw freethinkers whose ridiculous dogmatism did and does annoy me as much as the dogmatism of the orthodox. In fact, I respect the good Catholic more than the average freethinker.[15]

Indeed for Connolly, the intellectual heritage of freethought was a burdensome encumbrance on marxist theory, and one that was in principle contradictory to its basic teaching. Perceiving the origin of such beliefs in the ideology of the bourgeois French revolution, he observed:

> . . . such doctrines are the legitimate children of the teachings of individualism, and their first progenitors both in England and France were also the first great exponents of the capitalist doctrines of free trade and free competition, free contract and free labour. Such conceptions of religion are entirely opposed to the modern doctrine [i.e. marxism] that the intellectual conceptions of men are the product of their material conditions, and flow in the grooves channelled out by the economic environment.[16]

While freethinking characterises religion as a product of cynical and designing priesthoods, Connolly avers that the historical materialist method is able to achieve a genuine understanding of its nature. Even at its most popular level, it then appears as an expression of truth concerning the human condition in the natural world, which can be grasped by an undeveloped mind unable to handle abstract propositions. Connolly also stressed the value inherent in the development of consciousness from a pagan pantheistic mentality to a christian one. Such a spiritual development, he pointed out, was an essential feature of the modern individual's '. . . upward march to the conquest of truth'.[17] Connolly denied that socialist theory possessed the vision to judge the spiritual values and truth embodied in the religious consciousness. The marxist party, he wrote, was:

> . . . concerned only with the question of political and economic freedom for our class. We could not claim to have a mission to emancipate the human mind from *all errors*, for the simple reason that we were not and are not the repositories of *all* truth.[18]

Daniel De Leon, inflexible to the last in his own viewpoint, had Connolly hounded out of the SLP for his ideological heresy and condemned his concern for normative values by dubbing him 'an agent of the Jesuits'.

When in 1910, the year of Connolly's return to Ireland, *Labour in Irish History* was published, it was offered to the reading public, to use his own words, 'as part of the literature of the Gaelic revival'.[19] It was a work of marxist scholarship conceived both as a contribution to and a perception *within* that myriad antiquarian, historical, poetic, dramatic, athletic regeneration of Gaelic values in late romantic Ireland. In its context, the character of Connolly's history was fundamentally a metaphysical vision; a construct of speculative reason justified through empirical research technique, just as Marx's original concept of historical materialism had been. It was an historiography which defined Irish nationhood in terms of its self-revelatory practice through time: thus, the medieval Gaelic experience, the form of English conquest with Irish responses to it and a putative independent socialist republic, would all be 'moments' in this self-defining Irish historical drama. The *telos* of this drama, an established socialist political economy, would be the logical 're-conversion of Ireland to the Gaelic principle of common ownership by a people of their source of food and maintenance'.[20] On this material basis, the modern Gael would find it possible to realise the communal virtue embodied in the jurisprudence of his pagan forebears and the universal values of Irish Catholicity. Gaelic virtue had been obliterated and Catholic values compromised and degraded, by the alienating incursion of the English Right of Conquest with its accompanying proprietorial and capitalistic mores. Only the native proletariat – itself the product of the political economy of the conquest – embodied in its subject condition the will and the need to achieve a concrete and spiritual 're-conquest' of Ireland in the modern industrial age.

Catholicity was an intellectual and moral heritage which, although compromised to the point of disrepute in the bourgeois world, would yet be salvaged by and for the modern Gael *qua* revolutionary proletarian. Connolly's own work *Labour, Nationality and Religion* (1910) was both a pathology of the doctrine's moral demise *and* a reassertion of its basic value tenets in terms appropriate to the consciousness of the revolutionary proletariat. Indeed, towards the end of his life, Connolly was greatly encouraged by the stand taken by progressive members of the priesthood to bring the character of christian witness more closely in line with the needs of modern conditions. He rejoiced in the recognition that, substantively, their beliefs were congruent with those of Irish marxism, something that boded well for the future of Catholicity in Ireland. Commenting on a public lecture given by such a priest, the Capuchin Father Lawrence in January 1916, he wrote:

> . . . the reverend lecturer justly attributed the present position of the Church in France to the fact that Catholics in that country had wasted their time in dreaming of the impossible restoration of a monarchy instead of grappling with the practical work of social regeneration under the new conditions established by the republic. It is safe to say that such . . . [lectures as his] . . . are safer guarantees for Ireland against the growth here of anti-clericalism of the French type than would be all the pamphlets of the Catholic Truth society . . .
>
> . . . in all sincerity we could see no fundamental difference between the views expressed by Father Lawrence and those views we ourselves hold . . . The differences were apparently only differences of definition. The reverend lecturer called things by certain names, we would use totally different names, but in essence the things were identical.[21]

The details of the lost Gaelic heritage were quite another matter, and in Connolly's view could be retrieved only through scholarly research. Nor was it the empirical technique of historical materialism to which he looked for the answer, but the related methodology of positive sociology. Referring to Lewis Morgan's contribution to the sociology of early Mexico and Peru in his *Ancient Society*, Connolly opined, 'The same key will yet unlock the doors which guard the secrets of our native Celtic civilisation, and make them possible for fuller comprehension for the multitude.'[22]

Now this appeal to sociology contained in Connolly's foreword to *Labour in Irish History*, is an eccentric notion to discover at the outset of an avowedly marxist history. Sociology then, as now, affected an 'objective' scientific method totally free of the critical content of idealist philosophy which marxism later inherited. Free of such metaphysical principles by which existing social institutions might be judged (the core of marxist method) sociology is at base an apologetic rationale for the existing forms it seeks to describe. Nor was it intended to be anything other than this by its founder, Auguste Comte.[23] Connolly's ready acceptance of the character of pre-Norman Irish society as a classless, egalitarian civilisation – as suggested in his foreword – has been the target of consistent scholarly criticism of the work since it first appeared in 1910. He did not himself intend to deal with the period in his book and admittedly research in the field was then in its early stages. Certainly there is an element of truth in the judgment that this was one example of his desire to convince Irish workers of the radical dictates of their ancient past, leading him into one of the pitfalls typical of partisan nationalist writing.[24] However, the uncritical deference to sociological method may also indicate that he was in this particular regard caught up in the positivist mentality which – as we have noted – was a general feature of scientific socialism at the time.

With the mention of this element of positive science among some of the basic assumptions behind *Labour in Irish History*, it would be well now to recognise that *technically* Connolly's application of historical materialism was very orthodox and closely in conformity with the positive standards of the time. *Conceptually*, the scheme of the work is a demonstration of the history of the Irish nationalist movement and its ideology from 1649 to the point (Connolly's own time) when it might be capable of a logical accommodation with working-class interests in the form of marxist socialism. Technically, Connolly stressed, its method would be,

> to repair the deliberate neglect of the social question by our historians and . . . to demonstrate to the reading public the manner in which economic conditions have controlled and dominated our Irish history.[25]

This view is consistent with his description of marxism as an 'economic faith' (not being applicable to value questions such as religious issues),[26] and of its method as 'economic determinism'.[27] *Labour in Irish History* is not, nor was it intended to be, a sustained history of the Irish labour movement. Connolly himself described it as 'a record of labour in Irish History'.[28] In form it is a concordance to Irish history, a commentary illustrative of working and living conditions and of the political standpoint of the labouring people of town and country at the crucial conjunctures of modern Irish history. Its counterpoint style demands a thorough familiarity with the themes of modern Irish history on the reader's part if its message is to be grasped. An added difficulty of the work is its simultaneous attempt to reach two audiences. Parallel to the counterpoint critique designed to shake the faith of the initiated in the solidity of conventional historiography, runs a continuous attempt to dispel popular myth. This subtlety of approach and complexity of aim, together with Connolly's emphasis upon *consciousness* as an historical factor (and hence as an historiographical subject) all combine to make *Labour in Irish History* a unique historiographical achievement.

Prior to detailed examination of the book, it is worth recalling in full the stated proposition its argument seeks to justify. It runs:

> . . . in the evolution of civilisation, the progress of the fight for national liberty of any subject nation must, perforce, keep pace with the progress of the struggle for liberty of the most subject class in that nation, and that the shifting of economic and political forces which accompanies the development of the system of capitalist society leads inevitably to the increasing conservatism of the non-working class element, and to the revolutionary vigour and power of the working class.[29]

A determinist axiom then, at the outset: the identity of the working-class struggle with that of the struggle for Irish independence is declared absolute. There is, in addition, moral censure of those classes of Irishry who have accommodated themselves to the alien mores of the English proprietorial political economy. Thus the 'degenerate descendants' of the old chieftainry and the commercially motivated Baal-worshipping Irish capitalists are unregenerate supporters of the Anglo-Protestant ascendancy. By implication and extension, the working class remain the sole 'incorruptible' element in the Irish nation.[30] This moral purpose – combining Gaelic and christian notions of virtue – is of course the normative *sense* to the determined course of historical movement. Judgments of science and of value unashamedly, and necessarily, appear in tandem throughout *Labour in Irish History*.

For the period between the Williamite conquest (1691) and the heyday of the 'College Green parliament' in the 1780s, the first four chapters of *Labour in Irish History* must be read in conjunction with chapter 2 ('Ulster and the Conquest') of the *Reconquest of Ireland*. In this context, Connolly assaults several basic assumptions about Irish history which, in his view, are popular misconceptions which serve bourgeois interest both in the North and South of the country. These may be itemised thus: that the Irish supporters of James II in the 1690 campaign were a contemporary 'patriot' party: that the penal laws subsequently enacted against the Catholic population affected all classes equally: that relations in the North between landlords and tenants, 'planters' all, were harmonious and positive: that William's victory on the Boyne was one for Protestant-style liberation and a blow against a Catholic tyrant. The last point was most easily dispatched by recalling the diplomatic realities of the time: William's alliance with (among others) the Pope in the League of Augsburg, to curb the power of the Jacobites' chief source of aid, France. On landlord-tenant relations in the North, Connolly reminded his readers that, in Ulster, a predominantly presbyterian tenantry held their livelihood from prelatist landlords. These tenants-at-will had no security against rack-renting, nor power of constitutional redress against compulsory labour on public works. Far from living in a harmonious religious climate, they were harassed by recusancy fines and were excluded from public life and service (and the protection of the law) by test acts which were only repealed in 1780. Hence these Ulstermen were in a substantially similar situation to that of their Catholic countrymen in the South. The enactment of penal laws against Catholics was well known, but what was less well known, according to Connolly, was that wealthy Catholics were generally not harassed by these statutes, being tolerated for their financial strength and as valuable sources of loan capital for businessmen and improving farmers of either denomination. Tenants North and South, Catholic and Protestant, suffered equally in the famine of 1740, and were equally liable to rack-renting and eviction by improving landlords who were increasingly turning agrarian land to pasture towards the end of the period, to meet growing demands in England for dairy produce. On the Jacobite issue, Connolly was blunt indeed: stressing that both Jacobite and Williamite leaders were successive generations of land-thieves, each backing an *English* political faction to secure their property, he concluded the Irish people had no business shedding blood or treasure for either. Jacobite 'heroes' in Irish popular tradition such as Patrick Sarsfield, Connolly dubbed as little better than traitors for their actions in bringing war to a people who could nowise benefit from it.

Turning his attention to the period of the 'College Green parliament' dominated by the patriot party of Grattan and Flood, Connolly referred with some acidity to the belief – fostered by later constitutionalists among both Repeal and Home Rule parties – that such political 'freedom' had engendered great economic prosperity. Connolly characterised Grattan and Flood as cynical demagogues who contributed little to such prosperity as Ireland then enjoyed. This he traced to the Napoleonic wartime boom in trade with English markets; a period of commercial expansion based upon full exploitation of handicraft production. When manufacture became steam powered in the early nineteenth century however, Ireland, lacking the necessary resources (coal) inevitably felt a slump in activity. As an added point, Connolly recalled that there never were in operation at any time in Ireland discriminatory laws prohibiting any kind of industrial activity. Such a popular belief had been fostered by constitutionalists seeking to blame all evils upon the Union of 1800, he added.

Connolly gives little in the way of descriptive detail of the events of the United Irish rebellion of 1798 and its successor, the Emmet conspiracy of 1803. He stresses the trans-religious character of United Irish appeal and membership and the radical approach these revolutionaries took on social issues, following the democratic lines of the French republicans. He is silent however on problems such as Irish presbyterian feeling on the sheer statistical predominance of Catholics within the projected Irish republic, and also on Irish Catholic opinion concerning post-revolutionary Catholicism in France. The French church had been subjected to increased controls by the republican government, a secularist attempt which might not have been welcomed entirely by Catholic supporters of a putative United Irish republic, and not at all by the influential Irish clergy.[31] However, having stressed the internationalism of the United Irishmen and the support they received from the labouring poor (notably in the rural areas), Connolly takes up his main theme: the criticism of previous historiographical appreciations of them. These, he avers, are crippled either by suppressive hostility or by romantic, personalised treatment: in each case the *ideas* of the movement, and especially of its leader Theobald Wolfe Tone, have been largely ignored. Connolly's work seeks to redress the balance by allowing Tone and his comrades-in-arms to speak for themselves: fully three quarters of his chapter on the United Irishmen consists of direct quotation from their contemporary writings and manifestos in an attempt to make their ideas and example known to working-class Irish men and women of his generation.

The same concern motivates his treatment of Ireland's pioneer socialist theorist, William Thompson of Co. Cork (1775-1833) and of the experimental Owenite farming community at Ralahine, Co. Clare, in the 1830s. William Thompson, himself a landowner, published several works of political economy in the 1820s. Connolly interprets his position as mid-way between that of utopian and scientific socialism. It would perhaps be more correct to see Thompson as a radical political economist whose approach – utilising the empirical method of the classical analysts Smith and Ricardo – also took account of the social relations of production. Proceeding from the classical labour theory of value, Thompson pressed the view that the social subjection of labour was the prime cause of all economic misery and political instability, he addressed himself to the problem of a just basis of wealth distribution and formulated the (then highly radical) definition of capital as accumulated labour. Although he did not himself produce a general systematic theory for reform, his position could be seen as mid-way between classical political economy and marxist economics. The co-operative farm at Ralahine was established on declared Owenite principles in 1831 by a reforming and farsighted landlord. After several years of successful operation it was wound up only as a result of the landlord's own gambling misfortunes, when his creditors and mortgage-holders repudiated the community's lease. Using the original documentary and testimonial evidence, Connolly brings out the communal practice of the Ralahine society in terms of its governance, and the division of workload and distribution of its social product. In order to ensure a full equation of labour and value, a 'labour note' was used as the sole means of exchange between its members and in all its internal finance in place of regular currency. The harmony and efficiency of the experiment, together with its technological innovativeness, Connolly contrasts with the general agrarian situation in contemporary Ireland. With the much reduced demand in English markets for Irish products after the close of the Napoleonic wars, falling profits together with steady or increased rents had produced agrarian resistance which practically amounted to endemic civil war.

It was against this background of Ribbonite land war against tithes, rent increases and evictions, and of similar agrarian disturbances in Great Britian itself, that the public career of the great Daniel O'Connell was acted out. Instrumental in the winning of Catholic emancipation in 1829 and in creating the first mass movement in Irish history, O'Connell came to be idolised as a folk hero by his countrymen, as indicated by his sobriquet 'Liberator'. His faith in constitutional agitation for repeal of the Union as the ultimate redress for Ireland's calamities earned him the unstinting opprobrium of the radical nationalists of his generation, notably of John Mitchel, whose *Jail Journal* was a crucial seminal influence upon Connolly himself. Connolly's treatment of O'Connell owes something to Mitchel's contemporary vilification of the man, but the evidence marshalled in chapter 12 of *Labour in Irish History* denies any possible charge of his being captivated by traditional nationalist response. As in the case of the Jacobite Sarsfield and the parliamentarian Grattan, Connolly contends that O'Connell attached mass Irish political energies to a chimerical and bankrupt form of protest. Like them, he appears guilty of leading patriotic sentiment astray, while contriving in his own political behaviour to support a reactionary Whig government at Westminster. His inaction on the agrarian problem, his bitter hostility to labour legislation and to the working-class Chartist movement, and his own organisation's influence in suppressing the Irish Chartist groups, produce Connolly's inveterate criticism. Apart from these particular disservices to the cause of Irish labour, we may note a general achievement of O'Connell which, perhaps more than any other factor, accounts for Connolly's negative appraisal of him. O'Connell and his repeal association – like the Home Rule movement of Connolly's own day – sought to link the fortunes of the mass national movement in Ireland with those of English liberalism and with the existent (or, in O'Connell's case, emergent) British liberal state. As we have seen, it was the form and practice of nineteenth century Anglo-Irish liberalism which Connolly identified as the cardinal enemy of the cause of Irish labour.

After the failure of the Young Ireland 'Gironde' to organise popular Irish discontent during the disastrous famine years of 1847-49 into a genuine revolutionary attempt at armed rebellion (on account of their commitment to the private property principle), Connolly regards the cause of labour in Ireland as having reached the point of true self-consciousness; of developing its own independent and principled standpoint. In this connection, he instances the overwhelmingly working-class Fenian revolutionary brotherhood as a parallel to Marx's own International Workingmen's Association, and the latter day Land League of the quasi-socialist Home Rule leader Michael Davitt as a parallel to the emergent (reformist) labour democracies in the parliamentary systems of France and Germany. This independent, self-conscious stand he expected in his own day to issue in the organisation of a genuinely class-conscious marxist labour movement in Ireland, committed to a final act of proletarian-*cum*-national emancipation (the 'reconquest'). Above all, the opportunity for class-conscious action had to be *seized* by the proletarian leadership, and not allowed to be discounted in favour of constitutional niceties: he had, let us remember, chronicled in chapter 6 of *Labour in Irish History* just such a failure on the part of Irish capitalism to achieve a bourgeois revolution in the 1780s. The message of history became clear: whatever the circumstances, the Irish working class should on no account forfeit its mission to achieve the conditions of its own freedom.

Connolly sketched out in some detail the objective conditions of the Irish proletariat which impelled it to such a mission in his *Reconquest of Ireland* (1915). The scientific precision with which data pertaining to contemporary working-class conditions in Ireland is marshalled and analysed, almost for *measurable* revolutionary potential, recalls the technical competence of *Labour in Irish History*. However, in this sociological work, scientific (statistical) techniques of analysis clearly serve to forecast a determined course of events (revolutionary mobilisation). His historical work apart, it should be noted that Connolly was in some respects committed to a highly orthodox scientific-determinist mode of reasoning: this rather mechanistic approach is a parallel theme to the more reflective nature of his historiography, but it is no less noteworthy an element in his general materialist outlook. Examples of this mechanistic approach noted earlier are the theory of fully extended international capitalist development which precluded Irish industrialisation and his opposition to the De Leonist wage and price theory.*

A striking example occurs in chapter 8 of *Reconquest* on the question of the socialisation of agriculture. Connolly's views on agricultural organisation were totally in harmony with Marx's own 'big unit' ideal and, like Marx, he anticipated the inevitable end of peasant proprietary as an inefficient and outmoded form of production under maturing capitalism. Indeed his proposed agrarian policy differs little from that carried through (forcibly) in Soviet Russia in the inter-war period: nationalisation of land, to be effected by a collectivisation of holdings under a public administration. Large scale public investment would then fund the application of the latest technical advances to agriculture in the interest of general productivity. Central to the whole idea is the manifest vision that town-country divisions are fated to disappear and that agriculture is fated to evolve toward an industrial style of production.

Perhaps the best example of this kind of thinking in Connolly is in the area of imperialist relations and the related issue of war. Central to his approach is the conviction that England – as the most advanced capitalist country – must at all costs be prevented from extending its power and economic

*See chapter 1, pp.10–12 and chapter 2, pp.50–1 above.

longevity through further colonisation. If such colonisation continued, according to Connolly, other nations would fail to develop commercial and industrial capacity (and concommitant proletarian classes) and hence the progress toward socialism would be retarded. Connolly's view on the matter was a consistent one. As early as 1899 he wrote:

> Scientific revolutionary socialism teaches us that socialism can only be realised when capitalism has reached its zenith of development; that consequently the advance of nations industrially undeveloped into the capitalistic stage of industry . . . will breed a revolutionary proletariat in such countries and force forward there the political freedom necessary for the speedy success of the socialist movement; and finally, that as colonial expansion and the conquest of new markets are necessary for the prolongation of the life of capitalism, the prevention of colonial expansion and the loss of markets to countries capitalistically developed, such as England, precipitates economic crises there, and so gives an impulse to revolutionary thought and helps to shorten the period required to develop backward countries and thus prepare the economic conditions needed for our triumph.
>
> [hence] . . . every fresh conquest of territory by [English] armies, every sphere of influence acquired in the interests of her commercialists, is a span added to the life of capitalist society; and . . . every market lost, every sphere of influence captured by the non-capitalist enemies of England, shortens the life of capitalism . . .[32]

For these reasons, Connolly stated, he would '. . . welcome the humiliation of the British arms in any one of the conflicts in which it is at present engaged . . . '[33]

The same reasoning is evident in Connolly's response to the first world war more than a decade later. Writing in the *International Socialist Review* for March 1915, he detected the rise of German industry and commerce to rival that of England as the prime cause of the conflict. The trump card in the hand of British capitalism, he argued, had always been the British fleet, which was throughout modern history successively used to destroy the ocean-going commerce of every capitalist rival. He stated his plain belief that '. . . there is no hope of peaceful development for the industrial nations of continental Europe whilst Britian holds the dominance of the sea'. A British victory would confirm that dominance and would militate against '. . . that complete freedom of the seas by which alone the nations of the world can develop that industrial status which socialists maintain to be an indispensable condition for socialist triumph.' This mechanistic view helps in large part to comprehend the nature of the crisis faced by Connolly in 1914–16. He feared nothing as much as a British victory, since that would retard both international capitalism, and with it, the conditions for the growth of international socialism, for a future period of unknown duration. Scientism is above all else predictive and this preconceived economic macro-model was undoubtedly a rationale of long-standing in Connolly's mind. Connolly had once contrasted the bourgeois and socialist revolutions in terms of a general scientific principle as follows:

> The capitalist French revolutionist had to fight to destroy the institutions of his enemy: the socialist revolutionist has to fight in order to give the economic institutions of his enemy room to grow . . .[34]

Retrospect: Connolly's Revolution

Commitment to armed insurrection in the Easter Rising of 1916 was undoubtedly Connolly's ultimate political act. The meaning of such action, taken at such a time, cannot be readily deduced given Connolly's own reticence on his motivation. However, that action raises so many cardinal issues that it, equally, cannot be ignored. So then, the question remains: what kind of revolutionary act was Connolly's mobilisation for insurrection in 1916?

We have already found a few helpful hints in the foregoing argument. In part it was a response to war and to the possibility of a British victory which – on his mechanistic reasoning – threatened in principle the future growth of international capitalism and with it, the growth of international socialism. In a wartime situation it would not be unprecedented thinking on Connolly's part, for, as we have seen, he bruited a similar scheme of action at the height of the Boer war. His commitment to the marxist theory of the state was also a factor, since that view – regarding the state *as a function* of the class factor, rather than a reality independent of it – forced him toward a 'revolutionary defeatist' position. His correct theory on the state was of course syndicalist in orientation and expression; but no matter how erroneous this might be from a strict Leninist viewpoint, I would argue that it was, in principle, consistent marxist logic. Added to this is the obvious point Connolly himself made that genuine marxist politics could not be suspended during wartime, but must assume a practice appropriate to the changed conditions of struggle. As we have seen, Lenin himself, also acting as a consistent marxist, emphasised the same notion. Connolly's involvement in the rising clearly followed from his alliance with the extreme forces of cultural and romantic nationalism, as described above: England's difficulty might be Ireland's opportunity – a principle hallowed in the practice of the centuries-long Irish insurgent tradition. And it was, let us not forget, a possibility which occurred to him in advance of war's outbreak in connection with the unconstitutional arming of the Ulster Unionists to resist Home Rule by force or to at least forestall it by enforcing a partition of the country, to prevent its operation in the North.

All of this does outline a certain consistency of approach and continuity of principle in Connolly's responses, but it falls short of explaining 1916 as any kind of 'revolutionary act'. The key to the meaning of the act I believe to lie in the nature of the crisis which produced it, and the nature of that crisis as Connolly perceived it.

World war and Irish partition were, taken together, a gigantic crisis and one grievously aggravated by the weakness of international socialism generally and of Irish syndicalism particularly to take effective counteraction. And yet for all Connolly knew, the first world war might have passed off in similar fashion to the South African conflict: its end was certainly expected at an early date. As regards Home Rule, we have seen how Connolly had consistently argued against its acceptance as necessarily progressive in nature. I think we have to admit that he did not sacrifice his life – as he knowingly did before mobilisation that Easter Monday – on a straightforward anti-war/anti-partition basis. We must look deeper. I believe that whatever the war came to mean for Connolly about capitalism being in its death agony or not, it certainly meant the death agony of the *liberal state*. Capitalism might continue its course beyond the armistice, modified according to the needs of the hour, but it would not do so within the political framework of the liberal polity. In his last years, Connolly time and again stressed the fact that under wartime pressure civil and trades liberties had been obliterated with scant concern for any future restoration of constitutional norms. This argument is strengthened by reference to a very early warning from Connolly to the Irish working class that liberal constitutional freedom (and hence the freedom of the proletariat to mobilise for socialism democratically) is a transient phenomenon, an opportunity to be seized in the present before it might disappear in a problematic future. In the first edition (Dublin 1897) of *Erin's Hope*, Connolly called upon the Irish workers to organise at the polls in true reformist fashion to press for palliative measures (short-term improvements enforced by statute) '. . . while there is a rag of the constitution left'.[1]

To Connolly in 1914-15, there must have appeared precious few threads of the protective liberal constitution left, and in this regard we must remember his description of the capitalist class as a '. . . beast of prey [that] cannot be moralised, converted, or conciliated, but must be extirpated'.[2] The breakdown of the liberal state was also signalled by the Ulster crisis and especially the apparent powerlessness of the Asquith government to enforce its authority either upon the para-militarists of Carsons's movement or upon the 'Curragh mutineers' within the regular forces of the state. The final political breakdown had come and socialist organisation – notably the construction of strong class-conscious syndicalist bodies – had proceeded at too slow a pace to be able to meet it effectively. Connolly had analysed the failure on the part of European socialism to mount an anti-war effort in terms of *industrial* weakness, as we have seen: and what this observation amounted to was an admission that European socialism had been too 'late' – organisationally speaking – to meet the challenge of war. The 'backwardness' of the entire movement had been exposed in 1914 and this had precluded any attempt to seize the moment for revolutionary action.

So, in Connolly's view, both the Irish *and* the European movements suffered from a crippling backwardness from the advanced syndicalist or 'industrialist' perspective produced by the ultra-modern American movement. Focusing our attention more specifically on Ireland – as Connolly himself did in 1914-15 – it is obvious how much at variance the objective organisation of the working class was with the notion of conscious revolutionary unionism articulated by De Leonism. Put bluntly, it could be said that a syndicalist theory of revolution without a syndicalist organisation able to put it into effect is utopian. I believe Connolly had to face the cruel realisation of this radical dissonance between his theory and Irish (and European) realities at this critical conjuncture: it was his ultimate intellectual agony.

Nor could Connolly take any comfort that Irish backwardness would mitigate the political crisis in that country of the liberal state. Paradoxically Ireland's backwardness was highly complex; economic backwardness co-existed with political modernity in its dependent relation with the British state. Economically underdeveloped, 'backward' Ireland had played a full part in the bourgeois-democratic political system of the 'workshop of the world' since the union with Britain in 1800. Moreover, Ireland had, since the feudal period evolved co-extensively with England in terms of political practice, albeit usually with reluctance and usually with a dedication to sever the connection. In this perspective, Home Rule and partition were of a piece: both were attempts by different sections of the Irish bourgeoisie to give Ireland a backward polity (i.e. one without expensive, profit-cutting labour legislation, social services and the like) which would be in conformity with her backward economy. Both the Northern Unionist and Southern Home Ruler type of capitalist wished to impose in their different ways a nineteenth century statology dedicated to economic liberalism, upon early twentieth century Ireland. This is why Connolly inveighed against them and their ideologies as utterly reactionary.

The paradoxical reality of Ireland's political modernity is the conceptual base of Connolly's notion of revolution as expressed even as early as the 1890s in ISRP statements. We have noted above how – especially in *Erin's Hope* – he argued what might be called a 'no liberal state in Ireland' line. His evident distrust of Home Rule is based upon it and, as we have seen, throughout his entire career he persistently attempted (with little success) to warn British comrades against a principled commitment in support of the measure as 'progressive'. From the same concept, Connolly argued – again as early as the 'nineties – that a socialist government would have to precede full industrialisation in Ireland and that it would then organise production for use – autarky – and not for foreign competitive export. All of this thinking was an evident component of his 'Hibernicising' drive for an Irish road to socialism from his earliest days in Dublin and he did not change that thinking in any substantive respect subsequently.

The essential meaning of this thinking is that Ireland was *always* in his lifetime in a 'revolutionary' moment: there was always the possibility of seizing and acting upon a revolutionary opportunity. The means for doing so Connolly applied himself to assembling throughout his career – the creation of a genuine, historically-based, working-class consciousness and the organisation of that revolutionary will through syndicalist organisational method. His concept of the Irish revolution was not one of 'stages' such as might be appropriate to a situation of full backwardness in Russia and the colonised nations of Asia. His notion of working-class leadership of the revolution through political action did develop: initially he put his faith in the propagandist/reformist party (the ISRP) and later in the political (and ultimately the *military*) arm of the syndicalist OBU. The best comparison to be made is therefore with the Bolshevik notion developed by Parvus and Trotsky of the 'Permanent Revolution'.

1916, for all its shortcomings and Connolly's doubts, was an attempt – if a desperate one under extreme pressure – to seize the revolutionary moment in modern Irish history. The radical text of the Proclamation of the Republic reveals without mystery the ideal for which Connolly died. It was the socialist one, described in the proclamation in the admitted right 'of the people of Ireland to the ownership of Ireland', in its guarantee of 'equal opportunity' (in addition to liberal civil and religious rights) to all citizens and not least in its resolve 'to pursue the happiness and prosperity of the whole nation and of all its parts . . .'

For Connolly, the ultimate crisis of liberalism signalled *the* revolutionary moment. He could not, given the force of circumstance, strike at the precise time or in the exact way he would have chosen. But when he did he had reached the end of a road marked by consistency of principle and practice.

References

Introduction / pp.1-5

1. *Register of Births* (St. Giles, Edinburgh) 1868; Roll No. 605. C. Desmond Greaves in *The Life and Times of James Connolly*, London, Lawrence & Wishart 1972, pp. 20-23, was the first to bring to light the true facts of Connolly's birth.
2. No details of James Connolly's army service have survived, but since his elder brother John was given a military funeral in Edinburgh in 1916, it is known that he served as 20308 Corporal J. Reid, in the Royal Scots [Burial Record of Merchiston Cemetery, Edinburgh, 1916 – in the possession of Messrs. Wallace and Somerville, solicitors, Edinburgh].
C. Desmond Greaves, in *The Life and Times of James Connolly*, pp. 17, 20, 25-28, speculates that both brothers served in the King's Liverpool Regt. and on this basis adduces that James Connolly's period with the colours (assumed to be 1882-89) was spent at various stations in Ireland. Even if it is assumed that he followed his brother into the Royal Scots (the regiment which recruited then – as it still does – from the Edinburgh district), regimental movements for the period do not help locate him. Each regiment had at that time two regular battalions – a 'home' and an 'overseas' unit, the former constantly servicing the latter with replacements and reinforcements as the need arose. In support of the Greaves' thesis, it may be said that the 'home' battalion of the Royal Scots did serve in Ireland for two years of the period at issue (1882-84). For the remainder of the period till 1889, it was stationed in Edinburgh and Glasgow. [Regimental Movements, Royal Scots Museum, Edinburgh Castle].
3. Owen Dudley Edwards, *The Mind of an Activist – James Connolly*, Dublin, Gill & MacMillan 1971 p. 30.

1. The Hibernicisation of Marxism / pp.6-39

1. William O'Brien, *Forth the Banners Go,* ed. E. Maclysaght, Dublin, Three Candles 1969, pp.6-7.
2. A full account of Connolly's early career in the Edinburgh movement may be found in my thesis 'James Connolly and the Scottish Left' (Ph.D. Edinburgh University, 1975).
3. As suggested by O'Brien in *Forth The Banners Go*, *op.cit.* p.8 and C. Desmond Greaves in 'James Connolly – Marxist', *Marxism Today*, June 1968.
4. The full text of this 1896 programme is given in Desmond Ryan ed., *Socialism and Nationalism*, Dublin, Three Candles 1948 p.185.
5. James Connolly, *Erin's Hope* in Owen Dudley Edwards and Bernard Ransom eds., *James Connolly – Selected Political Writings*, London, Cape 1973, p.186.
6. *Ibid.* pp.178-180.
7. K. Marx and F. Engels, *Manifesto of the Communist Party*, Moscow, Progress Publishers 1967, p.44.
8. Edwards and Ransom eds., *op.cit.* p.180.
9. *Ibid.* p.187.
10. Harry Quelch, national secretary of the British SDF, said in 1893, 'Home Rule will be a victory the socialists can claim some share of' – *Justice* 20 May 1893.

11. Edwards and Ransom eds., *op.cit.* pp.173-74.
12. *Ibid.* p.176.
13. *Ibid.* p.173.
14. *Ibid.* p.176.
15. *Workers' Republic*, 13 August 1898.
16. Connolly in *Shan Van Vocht*, January 1897.
17. See Owen Dudley Edwards, 'Ireland' in Edwards, Evans, Rhys, MacDiarmid, *Celtic Nationalism*, London, Routledge & Kegan Paul 1968, p.143.
18. *Workers' Republic*, 17 June 1899.
19. *Harp*, September 1908.
20. *Catholic Times*, 22 November 1912.
21. *'Labour, Nationality and Religion'*, chapter 4 in Edwards and Ransom eds., *op.cit.* p.105.
22. Thomas Bell, *Pioneering Days*, London, Lawrence & Wishart 1941, p.51.
23. *Forward*, 3 May 1913.
24. *Ibid.*
25. *Ibid.*
26. Patrick O'Farrell, *Ireland's English Question*, New York, Schocken Books 1971, pp.269-70.
27. *Ibid.* p.268 ff.
28. *Catholic Bulletin*, November 1913, quoted in *O'Farrell, op.cit.* p.269.
29. *'Labour, Nationality and Religion'*, in Edwards and Ransom eds. *op.cit.* p.83.
30. *Ibid.* p.89
31. *Ibid.* pp.89-90.
32. *Ibid.* pp.91-2.
33. *Ibid.* pp.122-4.
34. *Ibid.* p.126.
35. *Forward*, 27 May 1911.
36. *Ibid.* 1 July 1911.
37. *Forward*, 23 August 1913.
38. *Forward*, 6 December 1913.
39. *L'Irlande Libre*, Paris 1897 - quoted in Ryan, *Socialism and Nationalism*, Dublin, Three Candles 1948, p.33.
40. *Forward*, 23 August 1913.
41. *Ibid.*

2. Syndicalism: Marxism-De Leonism and Beyond / pp.40-72

1. *Capital* Vol.3, Moscow, Progress Publishers 1961, p.379.
2. *Ibid.* p.431.
3. Henry Collins, 'The Marxism of the S.D.F.' in A. Briggs and J. Saville eds. *Essays in Labour History* (2), London, Macmillan 1971, p.55.
4. *Workers Republic*, 27 August 1898.
5. Letter from Connolly to the SLP of America, 31 March 1899. Quoted in C. Tsuzuki, 'The Impossibilist Revolt in Britain', *International Review of Social History*, I (1956), p.377.
6. Daniel De Leon, *Reform or Revolution*, Socialist Labour Press, n.d., pp.7, 14.
7. Karl Marx, *Critique of the Gotha Programme*, Moscow, Progress Publishers 1971, p.25.
8. *Ibid.* p.27.
9. *Ibid.* p.26.

10. *Workers' Republic*, 16 September 1899.
11. James Connolly, *Erin's Hope*, Dublin, ISRP 1897, pp.16-18.
12. James Connolly, *Erin's Hope*, New York Labor News Co. 1902, pp.48-9.
13. *Justice*, 25 May 1901.
14. *Socialist*, August 1903.
15. *Ibid.*
16. A full account of Connolly's role in the foundation of the British SLP may be found in my thesis '*James Connolly and the Scottish Left*' (Ph.D. Edinburgh University, 1975).
17. Connolly in *Weekly People*, 9 April 1904.
18. C. Desmond Greaves, *Life and Times of James Connolly*, London, Lawrence & Wishart 1972, p.176.
19. Karl Marx, *Value, Price and Profit*, Moscow, Progress Publishers 1970, p.50.
20. *Ibid.* p.51.
21. Connolly in *Weekly People*, 9 April 1904.
22. Manus O'Riordan, *Connolly in America*, Belfast, Irish Communist Organisation 1971, p.18.
23. Daniel De Leon, *The Burning Question of Trades Unionism*, S. L. Press, n.d. [1904] p.16.
24. *Ibid.*
25. O'Riordan, *op.cit.* p.53.
26. Marx and Engels *Manifesto of the Communist Party, op.cit.* p.61.
27. *Manifesto* of the Conference of Industrial Unionists at Chicago, January 2, 3 and 4, 1905: reprinted in Daniel De Leon, *The Socialist Reconstruction of Society*, S.L. Press, n.d., p.61.
28. *Ibid.* p.59.
29. George Lichtheim, *Marxism*, London, Routledge & Kegan Paul 1964, pp.222-24.
30. Paul Brissenden, *The Launching of the Industrial Workers of the World*, Berkeley, California U.P., 1913, p.38.
31. Daniel De Leon *The Socialist Reconstruction of Society*, pp.39-40.
32. *Ibid.* p.47.
33. *Ibid.* p.50.
34. *Ibid.* pp.48, 53-4.
35. *Ibid.* p.52.
36. Brissenden, *The Launching of the IWW*, *op.cit.* pp.31-5, 45.
37. *Ibid.* p.41.
38. 'The Future of Labor' in *Socialism Made Easy* in Edwards and Ransom eds., *op.cit.* pp.280–86.
39. *The Harp*, July 1908 in its editorial 'Political Action'.
40. 'Industrial Unionism and Constructive Socialism' in *Socialism Made Easy* in Edwards and Ransom eds., *op.cit.* p.273.
41. Connolly to J. C. Matheson of Falkirk, New York, 7 May 1908.
42. *Labour, Nationality and Religion* in Edwards and Ransom eds., *op.cit.* p.98.
43. *Socialism Made Easy* in Edwards and Ransom eds., *op.cit.* pp.272-3.
44. James Connolly, 'The Reconquest of Ireland' in *Labour in Ireland*, Dublin, Maunsel & Co. 1917, pp.327-8.
45. *Labour, Nationality and Religion* in Edwards and Ransom eds., *op.cit.* p.107.
46. *Socialist*, August 1903.
47. *Labour, Nationality and Religion*, in Edwards and Ransom, eds., *op.cit.* p.120.
48. 'Ballots, Bullets, or——', in *International Socialist Review*, October 1909.

49. *Workers' Republic*, 26 August 1899.
50. Connolly to William O'Brien, 12 September 1909.
51. 'Industrialism and the Trade Unions' in *International Socialist Review*, February 1910.
52. 'Socialist Party of Ireland – Its Aims and Methods', Dublin 1910.
53. Connolly in *Forward*, 1 October 1910.
54. *Syndicalist*, January 1912.
55. Edwards and Ransom eds., *op.cit.* p.24.
56. *Forward*, 10 May 1913.
57. *Forward*, 28 June 1913.
58. *Forward*, 23 August 1913.
59. *Forward*, 4 October 1913.
60. *Ibid.*
61. *Forward*, 10 January 1914.
62. 'Old Wine in New Bottles' in Edwards and Ransom eds., *op.cit.* pp.312-8.
63. *Forward*, 21 February 1914.
64. *Forward*, 23 May 1914.

3. The Crisis, 1914-16 / pp.73-91

1. *Forward*, 21 March 1914.
2. *Ibid.*
3. *Forward*, 28 March 1914.
4. *Forward*, 11 April 1914.
5. *Ibid.*
6. *Ibid.*
7. *Forward*, 18 April 1914.
8. 'The Irish Flag' in *Workers' Republic*, 8 April 1816.
9. *Forward*, 30 May 1914.
10. William O'Brien in Desmond Ryan ed., *Labour and Easter Week 1916*, Dublin, Three Candles 1949, pp.2-3.
11. *Forward*, 15 August 1914.
12. *Forward*, 22 August 1914.
13. *Ibid.*
14. V.I. Lenin, *The Collapse of the Second International*, Moscow, Progress Publishers 1969, p.15.
15. *Ibid*, p.37 ff.
16. 'Revolutionary Unionism and War', in *International Socialist Review*, Chicago, March 1915.
17. 'Our Disappearing Liberties' in *Workers' Republic*, 5 June 1915.
18. *Workers' Republic*, 22 January 1916.
19. A reference particularly directed against the social conservatism of Eoin MacNeill. He had remained unsympathetic to the ITWU's case in 1913 and in 1915 refused to lend the weight of the Volunteer movement to organised labour's campaign against economic conscription.
20. For a full description of the events and preparations which preceded the rising, Maureen Wall's two excellent articles should be consulted: 'The Background to the Rising . . . ' and 'The Plans and the Countermand . . . ' in Kevin Nowlan ed., *The Making of 1916*, Dublin, Stationery Office 1969, p.157 and p.201.
21. For its text see Edwards and Ransom eds., *op.cit.* p.377.
22. C. Desmond Greaves, *Life and Times of James Connolly*, p.420.
23. *Socialist Review*, September 1916.
24. *Lenin On Ireland*, Dublin, New Books 1970, pp.33-4.

4. Historiography and Scientific Materialism / pp.91-112

1. Friedrich Engels, *Ludwig Feuerbach and the End of Classical Philosophy*, Moscow, Progess Publishers 1969, p.55.
2. George Lichtheim, *Marxism*, London, Routledge & Kegan Paul 1964, pp.292-300.
3. Henry Pelling, *The Origins of the Labour Party, 1880-1900*, London, O.U.P. 1966, p.60. Joseph Clayton, *The Rise & Decline of Socialism in Great Britain, 1884-1924*, London, Faber 1926, p.30.
4. *Commonweal*, 12 October 1889.
5. John Glasse, *The Relation of the Church to Socialism*, Edinburgh, ILP 1900.
6. *Ibid.*
7. *Labour Leader*, 18 January 1896.
8. *Labour Leader*, 15 February 1896.
9. E. Maclysaght ed. *Forth the Banners Go* – reminiscences of William O'Brien Dublin, Three Candles 1969, pp.6-8.
10. *Socialist*, August 1903.
11. *Ibid.*
12. *Weekly People*, 9 April 1904.
13. Daniel De Leon, *Two Pages from Roman History*, New York Labor News Co., 1903, p.11.
14. Kautsky to Adler, 23 May 1902; quoted G. Lichtheim, *Marxism*, London, Routledge & Kegan Paul 1967, p.279.
15. Connolly to J. C. Matheson of Falkirk, 30 January 1908.
16. *Harp*, September 1908.
17. *Ibid.*
18. *Socialist*, June 1904.
19. James Connolly, *Labour in Irish History*, Dublin, New Books 1967, p.xxxi.
20. *Ibid.* p.xxx.
21. *Workers' Republic*, 29 January 1916.
22. Connolly, *Labour in Irish History*, p.xxxii.
23. H. Marcuse *Reason and Revolution*, London, Routledge & Kegan Paul 1969, pp.340-3.
24. Owen Dudley Edwards and Bernard Ransom eds. *James Connolly – Selected Political Writings*, London, Cape 1973, p.35.
25. Connolly, *Labour in Irish History*, *op.cit.* p.2.
26. James Connolly, *The New Evangel*, Dublin/Belfast, New Books 1968, p.34.
27. James Connolly, *Labour, Nationality and Religion*, Dublin, New Books 1969, p.20.
28. Connolly, *Labour in Irish History, op.cit.* p.128.
29. *Ibid.* p.xxxii.
30. *Ibid.* pp.xxxii-iii.
31. O. D. Edwards 'Ireland' in Edwards, G. Evans, I. Rhys, H. MacDiarmid, *Celtic Nationalism*, London, Routledge & Kegan Paul 1968, pp.74-5.
32. *Workers' Republic*, 4 November 1899.
33. *Ibid.*
34. *Socialist*, August 1903.

Retrospect: Connolly's Revolution / pp.114-118

1. Owen Dudley Edwards and Bernard Ransom, *James Connolly – Selected Writings*, London, Cape 1973, p.188.
2. *Workers' Republic*, 19 August 1899.

Index